Northwoods' Walleye

By Mike Mladenik
Professional Guide

Mike Mladenik   2011
N 6550 South 6th Street
Crivitz, Wi 54114

About The Author

Although smallmouth bass are my passion, a professional guide has to fish for the clients' preferred species and living in northern Wisconsin, walleyes are the staple for many guides. I am fortunate to guide in a place that has an abundance of prime walleye waters. The abundance of water allows a guide to choose the right water for any given day regardless of what Mother Nature throws at them.

In Northwoods Walleye, I follow the seasonal patterns for catching walleyes in lakes, reservoirs and natural lakes. The angler will learn the prime time to fish a specific type of water and choose the best presentation to catch those often finicky walleyes.

A guide soon learns to keep things as simple as possible so the client can have an enjoyable day on the water. Many anglers make fishing too complicated and end up catching less fish. Successful walleye fishing is neither complicated nor mysterious.

If you fish walleyes anywhere in North America, this book will help you put more fish in the boat. These tactics have worked for me for four decades and they should work for you.

Mike Mladenik

Table of Contents

Chapter One
The Basics

Walleyes are notorious for being persnickety. How many times have you been out on the water and had a slow day only to go to the landing and see another angler with a boat load of fish? Did the other anglers use some magic bait, use the right color jig, or just get lucky and stumble on a load of hungry walleyes? While they might have relied on luck, they were probably using the right bait for the right water and using it at the right time. While fishing is not an exact science, anglers need to understand the advantages and disadvantages of specific presentations.

Before we get into the issues of seasonal movements and walleye location, it is important to understand a few walleye basics. In this book I will be referring to certain walleye presentations and how they pertain to walleye movements. Some presentations will be specific and are only applicable to a certain time of year or type of water. Other presentations need to be refined to fit the type of water, weather conditions and period. Many times it is not the lack of walleyes, but the angler's poor choice of presentation that leaves them with an empty livewell. Anglers can also read too much into refining their presentation and make things way too complicated. I prefer to makes things as easy as possible whenever possible. Even though I will be going into further detail of walleye presentations in the upcoming chapter, I feel a basic understanding of a few presentations is in order.

Jigs

If there is one technique that a walleye fisherman can master that will put walleyes in the boat regardless of the season, it is the art of jig fishing. No walleye angler worth his weight in leeches can head out on the water without a tackle box full of jigs, but it is amazing how many of these anglers don't get it just right. An angler might have a ton of jigs, but do they have the right jig for the situation? The angler who is able to master the art of jig fishing knows what kind of jig to use under each situation. Here is a rundown of the basic types of jigs walleye fishermen use. If the average angler has a selection of these jigs in a variety of colors, they should be able to respond to almost any situation. Besides the profile of the jig, the hookeye location will dictate how the jig is retrieved.

Round jig – This is probably the most popular jighead and can be found in every bait shop in North America. The hookeye exits the top of the head, in excellent position for vertical presentation with the round head minimizing water resistance. Round jigheads are the most versatile jigheads since they work well with a cast and retrieve presentation and can be tipped with plastics or live bait. One major defect is that the round heads do tend to get hung up in weeds quite easily. If I had to choose only one jig style for any situation, it would be the round jighead.

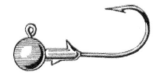 

Round Jig with barbed collar   **Round Jig with no collar**

The classic round jighead has a short collar of lead surrounding the hook shank. Thread a plastic grub onto the hook shank and slide it onto the collar to help hold it in place; barbed collars offer an even firmer grip to plastics. A ball or live bait head (no collar) enables you to thread a minnow directly up against the head, whereas a collar usually positions the minnow a bit farther behind the head. There are many modified roundheads on the market developed specifically for plastics.

River Jighead – This is a flat head style designed to slice down into the water. It sinks quickly and is excellent in the current. The hookeye is on top for vertical presentations.

Flat River Jig

Minnow/Darter Heads – These are pointier versions typically with a barbed collar or screwlock arrangement to be used with plastic grubs. The hookeye is on top and is used both for casting and retrieving as well as for vertical jigging.

Minnow Head

Darter Head

Standup Head – With the weight at the base of the jighead it creates a standup profile. The jig has the ability to hold a plastic bait tail or bait off the bottom, particularly with little tension on the line. The position of the hookeye is critical to the jigs' standup capabilities.

Pointed nosed standups with the hookeye forward, sticking out from the nose of the jig, tend to be more weedless-snagless; the line functions as a weedgard, with no place for weed fragments to become caught between the hookeye and the lead body. These jigs slip and slide through the weeds and are great for casting in shallow water, but create additional water resistance when fished vertically in deep water.

Standups with the eye exiting the top of the jighead are better suited to vertical presentations. They tend to hang up a bit in the weeds due to the eye position, but they crawl over rocks.

Stand Up Jig

Banana Jig – Curved or semi-standup heads with the hookeye positioned at the nose are used to slip across the bottom without snagging. They are good for shallow to moderate depths and horizontal presentations. The hookeye position at the nose lifts the jig nose first, creating resistance in all depths.

Banana Jig

Weedless Jigs – These jigs feature a wire or plastic weedguard with the hookeye emerging from the nose. They are deadly in weeds but many walleye anglers frown on weed guards.

Most walleye anglers use six foot six or seven foot medium or medium light action rods when jigging. The shallower the water and the lighter the jig the lighter the rod action should be. When jigging deep water with heavy jigs you might need to go to a medium heavy action rod.

Slip Bobber Basics

I have been using bobbers for as long as I have been fishing. When the word bobber comes to mind most anglers reminisce of their childhood. I for example would sit by the bank and wait anxiously for a fish to suck in my nightcrawler

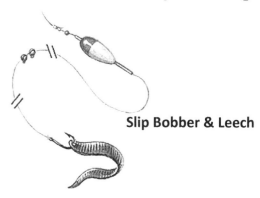

Slip Bobber & Leech

and submerge my bobber. Some days I would get a strike as soon as the bobber hit the water, but more often than not, I would watch the bobber for a while and my mind would begin to wander. I was not bored with fishing, but just bored with watching the bobber.

So after a short time, I would grab another rod and make fierce casts with an in-line spinner or crankbait. I would cast in every direction getting snagged on trees and weeds, but it did keep me occupied, and even if I didn't catch anything I was happy. Usually, the only fish that I would catch in my young years was on the live bait and bobber. If I did catch a big fish I would often tell people that I caught it on the lure and not the worm. I guess that fishermen learn at an early age to stretch the truth.

For years, it seemed that I had developed an aversion to "bobber fishing" and refused to use them. Even though I knew it worked, it just wasn't cool. Bobbers were for kids and old people and not fishermen who know what they were doing. Well, after I grew up and started guiding, I finally realized what a deadly weapon a bobber was and what a fool I was not to have used them. Even to this day, I still run across a few walleye anglers who are too proud to fish with a bobber. Well, if they choose their false pride over catching fish that is their problem, not mine.

Over the years slip bobbers have enabled me to catch walleyes, smallmouth bass, largemouth bass, northern pike and panfish. If fished effectively, a slip bobber will enable an angler to catch walleyes from spring through ice up. Granted, the slip bobber techniques that I use today are a far cry from my childhood memories. In my younger years the only thing I worried about was that the bait stayed on the line when I made my cast. Compared to those early years of my childhood, fishing with a slip bobber has evolved into a science.

Mastering the art of slip bobber fishing is not all that difficult as long as an angler follows a few basics. The biggest reason for a slip bobbers' effectiveness is the ability of the angler to place the bait in the strike zone with ease. Prior to slip bobbers if the angler wanted to fish his bait at eight feet, he had to cast the entire eight feet of line with his bobber and bait attached. Most of the time the angler would make a power cast to get distance and the bait would fly off the hook. This technique was difficult for an adult to master let alone a kid. Prior to slip bobbers anglers tossed out bait a few feet below the bobber and let it sit there, just hoping for a bite. Everything looked good, except for the fact that the fish was sitting three feet below the bait and refused to move.

Rigging up the slip bobber is easy since there are several pre packaged rigs on the market. When setting up the rig, place the tube with the knot on your line, slide the knot off the tube and pull the tag ends of the knot tight and trim off the tag ends. Next, place a bead on the line and then thread the bobber on the line. Place a few split shots on the line and tie on a live bait hook or a jig and you are good to go. With a slip bobber the angler uses a movable nylon knot, which you can purchase pre-tied, that you put on your line to stop the bobber. The bobber itself is hollow so it can slide

A spinner rig is made up of line, clevises, beads, blades and floats combined with live bait to catch walleyes in a variety of situations. The blades and beads emit both noise and color and can be a very effective in triggering a strike from a neutral or inactive walleye. They have evolved over the years and on many days changing a blade color or bead can mean the difference between catching a couple of walleyes or a boat load.

Line - Most spinner rigs are tied with line heavier than 10 pound test. The theory is that too supple a line will wear and will not be tough enough to be pulled through various situations. Most pre-tied rigs are tied with a minimum of 17 pound test.

Hooks - Some anglers prefer a 2-4 Aberdeen style hook when using minnows. For leeches and nightcrawlers a number 4 or number 6 octopus style hook is the most popular. Actual hook types will depend on the individual angler. The new color-coated hooks have become popular in recent years.

Octopus Hooks

Clevis – Some waters are easy to pattern and when fished with one or two types of blades metal clevises will work well. However, on some waters you will need to fine tune your blades throughout the day. If this is the case, the plastic clevis will allow the angler to change blades accordingly.

up and down to your bait, and not interfere with your casting. As you reel in your line the knot will past through the rod guides and onto the reel. This will allow the angler to cast with the bobber one to two feet from the rod tip helping to insure an accurate cast.   When the bobber settles on the water, your bait will ride down and remain at the exact depth.

Deciding on whether to tie on a hook or a jig to present the bait will depend on the conditions and walleye activity level. In calm conditions a quality plain hook works best. If using a leech or nightcrawler I use a size four or six hook. When using a minnow, go to a larger hook that will match the size of the minnow. When using a minnow, if the hook is too small you won't get a good hookset. Some anglers like to use colored hooks, which can trigger a strike. If there is a good chop on the water a plain hook will still work, but a light jighead is preferred by many anglers. The jig head will add both action and color to the presentation.

One's choice of rod when fishing a slip bobber is very important since the right rod will aid both casting distance and setting the hook. Anglers who have trouble hooking walleyes when using a slip bobber often blame missed fish on the light bite. The number one reason for missed wall-eyes is the angler's choice in fishing rod. I feel a seven foot medium light action rod is ideal for most people, although some anglers prefer a slightly longer rod. A lighter action rod will help absorb the cast. If the rod is too stiff anglers will have a tendency to jerk the rod on the cast and you won't reach the desired target. The lighter action rod will also allow for a softer hookset and will result in more hooked walleyes. I usually spool my reels with six pound test monofilament or fluorocarbon/mono hybrid line.

Beads – The size and type of bead are both important considerations. Much of the "dialing in" of a rig to a specific fishery involves imitating forage and its colors. A fishery with lots of perch will require more yellow, blacks and some reds. But if the fishery contains ciscoes or whitefish, it will require the use of white, pearl and silver beads. Generally, a 4mm bead is a good start with a 6mm being a large bead. The angler also has the option of glass, plastic, multifaceted and plain opaque beads. Some beads even contain rattles for dark turbid water.

Blades – Although the color of the blade is important, the style of blade will have an impact on the sound that is emitted. A hatchet style blade for example will chop and displace more water, giving off more underwater sound/ vibration. On the opposite end of the spectrum, a willow leaf blade doesn't give off a great amount of sound or vibration. The size of the blade is also very important. In some instances, only one size is attractive to walleyes and thus effective. Early season walleyes seem to show a preference towards smaller blades while late fall walleyes are attracted to larger blades. Color choice is important, especially for matching forage and visibility in dark water.

Floats – Floats are used to lift the spinner. Even though the spinning blade will lift the rig, if worked at a slow speed it will drag the bottom. The float will lift the rig even at slow speeds and create a larger visual profile.

Typical Spinner Rigs

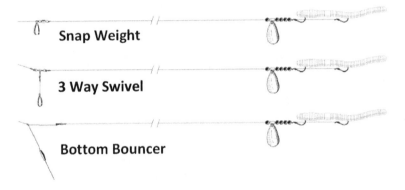

Snap Weight

3 Way Swivel

Bottom Bouncer

Crankbaits

Casting and trolling crankbaits is a good way to locate walleyes. You can cover water faster with a crankbait than with any other presentation. While my expertise with trolling is very limited, I have caught a considerable number of walleyes casting crankbaits. When casting crankbaits it is important to try to match the preferred walleye forage. This does not necessarily mean matching the color of the forage so much as attempting to match the profile of the forage. A crankbait is best cast around cover or to a depth where it just bounces off the bottom.

The same crankbait rods that are used by bass anglers are also in order when casting crankbaits for walleye. A longer seven foot or seven foot six rod will allow you to make maximum casts and keep the crankbait in the strike zone for the longest amount of time. One problem that can arise is that walleye anglers tend to use the same rods for trolling and casting crankbaits. Trolling rods are longer and have a slower action. Line type is also an important consideration. Fluorocarbon line will sink which also aids the crankbait in reaching its maximum depth.

Favorite Walleye Crankbaits

Rapala Shad Rap   **Yo-Zuri Crank'n Shad**

Yo-Zuri Crystal Minnow

Over the years I have fished with just about every lure and live bait that has ever been concocted. Some have worked while others have raised a question in my mind as to why anyone would ever remotely consider using them. While all these modern innovations are great, I must admit that when it comes to catching walleyes, I rely on one basic presentation as my go to bait. When the fishing is tough, as it often can be, it is hard to beat a hook and a leech or nightcrawler. A number four live bait hook tied on the end of six pound test monofilament or hybrid line and a small split shot clinched two feet up from the hook will catch fish when all else seems to fail.

Keep It Simple!

Jig & Grubs For Walleye

Walleye options

Hair Jig

Chapter Two
Spring River Walleye

    Winters can be long in the upper Midwest, and the craving for open water can drive anglers like me to almost lose what little sanity they have. While ice fishing is fine for many anglers, it is still not the same as casting into open water. In my younger days, I have been known to crawl over snow banks in sub zero temperatures just to make a cast below a dam in mid-January. Most of the time I would not catch anything, but it was a temporary fix.

    Occasionally, fishing open water in the winter can be productive but conditions have to be just right. Many years ago I had an exceptional day fishing open water in late February when most ice fisherman were getting skunked. In fact, the reason I tried the open water was that the ice fishing was so poor. I had fished a flowage for several nights during a warming trend and had not caught a single walleye.

a) The warm February continued and since the walleyes were not biting on the flowage, I decided to take a ride and enjoy the nice day. I stopped on a bridge and gazed at the water and suddenly it hit me: the walleye season is open until the end of February and hook and line fishing in open water is legal. As I gazed at the minimal current, I locked in several places that could hold walleye. I headed for home to reload, tossing my pail full of tip ups into the corner; deciding that I would worry about them the next winter.

I returned back to the bridge, and found a place where I could wedge my truck between two snow banks so it was off the road. I put on my waders and with one fishing rod, a small box of jigs, curly tail grubs and about a dozen fathead minnows, I headed over a snowbank to open water. The snow had started to melt due to the mild weather and long February days, making my journey to open water quite effortless, of course, this was prior to surgery to have two knees and one hip replaced.

As I approached the river, I had to make a commitment as to where the best place to fish would be. Not the most comfortable place mind you, but the place that would hold at least one hungry walleye that would become my supper. I chose to fish a deep hole completely out of the current on the back side of a rock ledge. Not only did it look fishy, but with the cold water and lack of current, I was certain walleye were present. The mild February had also contributed to a lack of snow along the bank allowing me to easily slip into the water within easy reach of my minnow bucket.

Once in the water I tied on a 1/8 ounce chartreuse leadhead jig and tipped it with a fathead minnow. Knowing that no walleye would be found in the current I made my first cast right in the deep water, letting it fall slowly to the bottom. I reeled in the slack line and lifted the jig and felt a hard thump which turned out to be nothing more than a rock or possibly a northern pike. Anyway, it surely was not a walleye.

Figuring that the chartreuse jig was the cause of my snag, I opted to tie on an orange jig and made my next cast slightly upstream from the hole right on the edge of the current. The jig and minnow again began to fall and I again felt a hard thump. This time I set the hook and experienced a slight movement in my line. Next, the line seemed to stop and I felt nothing on the end of the line. I slowly reeled in about a foot of line and again felt life on the end of the line. It did not feel like a big fish but I knew that in the cold water it is impossible to tell for sure.

After a slow steady pull in a short time I grabbed a slim walleye out of the cold water. While far from a legal 15 inch walleye, I was excited, since it was bigger than any walleye I had seen in the past month while fishing on hard water. With adrenaline flowing, I quickly tipped the orange jig with another fathead minnow and tossed into the same location in hopes of a walleye a few inches larger.

My cast was perfect and as the jig fell off the rock ledge and hit the bottom I again felt a hard thump. With a slow sweep of the rod it was evident I had connected with another walleye. While it felt a bit larger, it did not feel like there was anything to get excited about. However, once I saw the fish it was evident that it could be a legal fish. As I picked the walleye out of the water it occurred to me that I had no way to measure the walleye. Now, being a guide, I had handled many walleye and can guess the size of a fish as good as anyone. But a guess is a guess and having no way to verify the length of the walleye I released my supper.

I had definitely found the honey hole as I continued to catch and release five more walleye that were close to or slightly over the 15 inch mark. Thinking the walleyes were active, I made several casts with curly tail grubs in a variety of colors but could not connect with another walleye. So I Returning to the jig and minnow combination, I tried in vain to catch another walleye.

Stepping back on the shoreline, I decided to go farther downstream where I knew there was a deeper hole, hoping to find a few walleyes large enough that they would meet the 15 inch measurement required to keep them. With minimal current and low water it was easy for me to maneuver along the shoreline. I was familiar with the river since I had fished the hole several times from a boat. There was a ledge similar to the one I had fished before with the exception being that the hole was 8-10 feet deep.

I made a few casts without either a fish or a snag and decided to upgrade to a ¼ ounce orange jighead. On my second cast I felt a thump and slight movement on the end of the line. As I set the hook it was evident that if it was a walleye there would be no need to measure it. The fish felt heavy and for a while I thought it was a northern pike. However, after I saw the white tip of the tail I knew it was not only a walleye, but a large walleye at that. While I knew it was a legal fish, I could see it was a big female loaded with spawn. I estimated the walleye to go about 26 inches as I turned her loose. I might want a walleye dinner, but I can't see keeping a prime spawning fish a few months prior to the spawn. My interest in practicing good conservation outweighed my interest in a walleye fillet for supper.

I looked in my minnow bucket and I had two minnows left. On my next cast I got hung up in the rocks and decided that this time it was the fault of the orange jig, so I decided to use up my last minnow with a yellow jig. After a few casts I again connected with a walleye that was at least the size of the fish I had just released. If I did not know better, I would have thought it was the same walleye. Anyway, I was out of minnows and had already established that they would not hit a jig and curly tail grub.

It was a great day on the water, especially after getting skunked for several days. While I caught lots of fish I went home without a meal. I was certain that a few of the walleyes that I had caught were over 15 inches, but I could not be sure. The lesson learned was to always bring along some sort of measuring device when fishing for walleyes.

I continued to fish open water below dams in late winter when the conditions allowed, but never had the success that I had that warm February day. On occasion I had caught good numbers of walleye but never that many large walleyes. By taking advantage of the late February bite I am able to fish waters that otherwise would not be open until the Wisconsin Spring Opener, which is the first Saturday in May.

In the upper Midwest the Spring Walleye Run is a tradition. Anglers have many options open for spring walleyes. Many river systems have continuous open seasons that give anglers the chance to bring home both a trophy walleye and a few fish for a meal. Regulations can vary not only from state to state but from specific stretches of river. Some river sections are managed as trophy fisheries while others have restricted bag limits so be sure to check the regulations.

To successfully catch spring river walleyes, anglers need to be aware of the present conditions. Water temperature, water levels, prevailing weather and current are all critical for both walleye location and presentations. Once you establish a pattern don't make the mistake of getting in a rut. Spring is known for changing conditions and as the conditions change so do the patterns. The faster you adapt to change the more fish you will catch.

It is no secret that walleyes and walleye anglers will concentrate below dams in spring. While fishing below dams can be very productive it can also be tough fishing. It is surprising how many anglers don't fully understand the way all fish relate to a dam. In spring, many anglers will toss out the anchor and start fishing without analyzing the current situation. Adapting your presentation to the current will make the difference from a few fish to steady action.

Over the years I have had my best success fishing on the edges of the main current flow. Not only does the current break attract fish but with less current the fishing will be easier. Walleyes relating to faster current will hold tighter to the bottom and you will literally need to drop a jig on their nose to trigger a strike. The swifter the current the tighter the large walleyes will be holding to the bottom. You may find the largest fish in this area but fishing for them can be frustrating.

I have found that current breaks below a dam tend to be a holding area for both pre-spawn female and male walleyes. It is common to catch a few small walleyes and suddenly stick a big female. What happens is that larger fish are on the move and will use the current edge as their direct route to the spawning areas. Spawning areas in the vicinity of a dam can include rubble, gravel or other hard bottom.

Both a jig and minnow or a jig and plastic trailer are effective. When choosing plastics I use both curly tail grubs and shad style baits. If the walleye are active the jig and plastic is easier to use. However, if the bite is light I rely on a jig and shiner or a large fathead minnow. Cast upstream towards the shoreline and the slack water area and slowly retrieve the jig into the current. Once the jig enters the current break I raise my rod tip to about 10 o'clock and keep a tight line. If you detect a strike, lower the rod slightly and then set the hook.

During this early walleye season the shore angler has the advantage. Most of the boat landings are still iced over but you have plenty of open water below the dams. Before river levels rise with the spring runoff walleye can be stacked below the dam. Current is minimal at this time and a light jig tipped with a grub or shiner is deadly.

The advantage shore fishing has is that you can fish several dams on the same day. If you fish below one dam and can't seem to connect with fish take a drive and move to the next dam. I have done this on several occasions until I found active walleyes. Current flow below the dams can change on a daily basis and can change walleye location and activity.

When fishing from shore I prefer to use at least a seven foot rod. Even longer steelhead rods can be effective. You will need to make long casts and cover as much water as possible. Make sure the rod is both sensitive enough to detect a strike and stiff enough for a good hookset.

While fishing from the shore is indeed a productive method for catching spring walleyes it is hard to beat a boat. Toss in some high water, which is notorious in spring, and shore fishing for walleyes can be dangerous if not impossible. As a rule of thumb I prefer to fish from shore early in the season but as the season progresses I rely on my boat. The mobility of a boat will allow anglers to locate large numbers of pre-spawn walleyes regardless of the weather and river conditions.

Fishing below dams in spring is one of the most popular methods of early season walleye anglers. However, that usually results in crowds, and not being a fan of crowds I choose to fish elsewhere. While I might have to work a bit harder to locate walleyes, when they are found you will find them in large numbers, and a trophy walleye is always a possibility.

One of the biggest misconceptions about the spring walleye run is that all the walleyes will spawn below a dam. To be sure, below any given dam on a northern river there will be a degree of spawning walleye activity. Trying to avoid the crowds over the years made it evident that I would have to avoid fishing below a dam in the spring. Sure there is lots of water in a river, but the key is to find productive water, especially if you expect to remain a fishing guide. Over the years, I have made my living not fishing below dams, but concentrating on river sloughs.

The ideal slough will have a few key elements if it is going to attract spawning walleyes. After many years of experience, the first thing I look for is a slough that is on an edge of the bend of a river. By being on the bend of the river the angler is assured that there will be a deep hole adjacent to the slough. The river bend will also create natural current breaks along with the many logs and debris that have moved down river over the years. If the slough is not adjacent to a bend in the river it will attract a few walleye but not large numbers.

However, the best looking slough will not attract

spawning walleyes if there is no place around the slough where walleyes can spawn. Many sloughs are entirely muck bottom and may attract pike, rough fish and pan-fish, but no walleyes. This is a common scenario even on the best walleye rivers in the upper Midwest as anglers find one slough filled with walleye and another a few miles downriver won't attract any walleyes.

A slough will hold walleyes not only during the spawn but during the pre-spawn and post spawn as well. Not only will these areas attract large numbers of early season walleyes but they are predictable. Regardless of the river conditions, walleyes will be present, and all the angler has to do is adapt to the water levels and prevailing weather conditions. It is easier to figure out a fishing pattern once you have located walleyes as opposed to just plain trying to find walleyes.

The ideal slough will of course be on the bend of a river and have a small creek entering into the slough. The creek itself can be the main focal point for walleye spawn-ing. If the creek is large enough walleyes will enter the creek to spawn. How far the walleyes will move into the creek will depend on the creeks' depth and bottom con-tent. On a small creek if gravel or rubble is present wall-eyes will spawn at the mouth. However, on a larger creek walleye may travel upstream until they find a suitable hard bottom to spawn.

On one of my favorite sloughs that I have fished successfully for years, walleyes will spawn in the creek during high water but when the water is low they spawn as far as 5 yards away from the creek. On one side of the creek there is a small rock island just on the edge of the main river current. Under low water conditions the wall-eyes will stack up and spawn along the edge of the island. It is important to keep in mind that river walleyes use the current when spawning and although they usually spawn in the same general area, the actual current will dictate spawning location.

Prior to spawning, big female walleyes will stack up in deep water on the edge of the slough. Deep water can be only six or seven feet on the edge of one slough and as deep as 20 feet at another slough. The shallower water is easier to fish but anglers will need to be a bit more stealthy since the large walleyes are easily spooked. These walleyes can be very aggressive, but catching one big walleye can turn the other off. On overcast days look for the big walleyes not to be quite as gun shy. Deeper water will take more patience to work your presentation on the bottom, but you have a better chance of catching several big walleyes. In fact, on one April day my clients and I boated 8 walleyes over 20 inches right in the middle of the day.

When fishing shallow water on the edge of a slough I rely primarily on a jig and minnow. If the water temperature is below 40 degrees, I use a plain leadhead jig with a minnow. In stained river water my favorite jig colors are orange, chartreuse, hot pink and yellow. Once the water temperature climbs over 40 degrees I like to tip the jighead with both a three or four inch curly tail grub and a minnow. I usually bring along both river shiners and fathead minnows. While a big walleye will hit a fathead minnow in spring, a river shiner will trigger a strike from a neutral walleye. The only problem with shiners is that they don't survive after a few casts. So avoid hard fast casts and opt to flip the jig and minnow. In the shallow water, vertical jigging can be tough on these spooky walleyes so I either anchor and cast the edge of the slow or if possible use my electric trolling motor to position my boat just within casting distance of the edge of the slough.

The same jig and minnow presentations will work in deeper water but you will need to experiment with the size of your jig. If possible, depending on the current and wind, I prefer to vertical jig over the walleyes as opposed to anchoring. Vertical jigging will allow you to position the boat directly over the marked walleyes.

Many walleye anglers rely heavily on vertical jigging but others never really master the technique. If the angler does not keep the line vertical, you will not connect with many, if *any* walleyes. Use your bow mounted trolling motor to hover slowly over your targeted area, slipping slowly downstream, slightly slower than the current. Keep in mind that the current on the bottom, where the walleyes are holding, is slower so you will need to adjust your slipping speed accordingly. Depending on the depth of the water, you can use anywhere from a quarter ounce to a half ounce jig, so bring lots of jigs along.

Vertical jigging caught this big walleye

It is important to watch both your line and rod tip since often times a strike can be hard to detect. Too many of my clients want to set the hook home with the slightest twitch of the rod or rod tip and they end up fishless. One tip I give my clients is to test the bite before setting the hook. If you feel any resistance on the line, raise your rod tip a few inches. The trick is to confirm the bite before the walleye feels pressure and drops the bait. This will take patience and persistence, but if you master this technique I guarantee you will catch more walleyes.

One reason anglers have trouble mastering vertical jigging is due to their poor choice in rod. If the action of the rod is too slow you won't be able to feel bottom contact. I tell my clients to let the jig ride 1to 4 inches off the bottom, and with the bottom usually being erratic, if they are in contact with the bottom too long they will get snagged. A lighter action rod will allow you to feel the bottom quicker and besides avoiding snags it will keep you at the desired depth. A six foot or six foot six light action rod is ideal. The light action rod will also be a plus in detecting light pickups.

Another presentation that has caught many big wall-eyes over the years, especially under tough conditions is a floating crankbait fished on the bottom. The only way you can fish this rig wrong is to move it too fast. First off, attach a slip sinker on your line and tie on a quality barrel swivel on the end of your eight pound test monofilament, braided or hybrid line. Next, attach about three or four feet of six or eight pound fluorocarbon leader, then at-tach a three or four inch floating minnow imitation crank-bait.

You will need to experiment with both your slip sinker weight and your crankbait. The weight will sit on the bottom but your crankbait will ride a few feet off the bottom. The current will give the crankbait a slow movement as is sweeps from side to side. The longer your leader is the longer your sweep will be but if you are dealing with a restricted area you will need a shorter leader. The color of the crankbait that you choose will depend on water color. If the water is stained with only fair clarity I prefer black/silver or a highly reflective crankbait. If the water is heavily stained, brighter fluorescent crankbaits are preferred. Regardless of the water color the more reflectivity in the crankbait the greater your odds are to trigger a strike. A floating crankbait that rattles will also occasionally trigger a strike.

Due to the current and the fact that the crankbait is floating, you do not need to do much. In fact, my advice is to set the rod on a rod holder and jig with another rod. This is one of the few times when I advocate fishing with an unattended rod. However, keep an eye on the rod since due to the treble hooks on the crankbait, a walleye is easily hooked. You will seldom have missed fish with this technique. The only negative thing about this rig is it does not work well if the bottom contains a lot of wood. Both the sinker and the crankbait will snag easily.

Bridges are notorious for attracting large pre-spawn walleye. You won't catch the most fish around a bridge but you might catch the largest walleye of the day. While all bridges are different, most have a few things in common. A bridge is a neck down area that funnels through any fish heading upstream or downstream. Another factor they have in common, regardless of the size of the bridge, is that a deep hole and hump are usually in proximity of the bridge. These are key factors in attracting and holding big walleyes.

As walleyes head upstream on the spawning migration in the cold water, the increased current around the bridge can add stress on a big female walleye. Walleyes will move deeper and stage in the hole or behind a hump to avoid the current. The swifter the current the tighter walleyes will hold to the bottom which can make them difficult to mark even with good electronics. There have been many times when I have caught big walleyes from a bridge hole when my locator marked no fish.

One spring I had a client boat a 30 inch walleye during the most deplorable weather conditions. We had a front move through two days prior to our outing and to make matters worse the already high river had to absorb a few more inches of rain. Due to the rising water and 40 degree air temperature, not to mention the brisk northwest wind, I knew the walleyes would be holding tight. Need-less to say, as a guide I knew I had my work cut out for me.

We fished four hours without a strike and both of us were about ready to call for an early quitting time. I suggested that we try the bridge that we had fished earlier one more time since it was on the way back to the boat landing. Even though we had no action at the bridge earlier in the day, I assured my client that it was possible a few fish could have moved into the hole. He gave me the nod and I only hoped there would be at least one foolish walleye dumb enough to venture off the hole under these deplorable conditions.

With the swift current and northwest wind, I knew it would be tough to try to anchor and impossible to hold with a trolling motor or outboard. However, this bridge was low enough that I could tie off on the beam of the old railroad bridge. After I tied off the boat I told my client to tie on a 3/8 ounce chartreuse leadhead jig, tip it with one of the larger shiners in the minnow bucket and cast slightly upstream on the right hand side of the boat.

He made several fan casts in all directions and we came

to the conclusion that he had thoroughly fished the hole. He insisted that he make a few more casts but he wanted to change the jig. I suggested he tie on either an orange or hot pink jig and he chose the orange one. He made two casts without a strike but on the third cast his rod bent over and we both knew it was not a snag. The drag on the reel began to scream and both of us jumped out of our comfortable seats. All of a sudden the cold and wind did not seem to be a problem as I watched the excitement in the face of my client. The fish made a few runs and we still had not established its ethnicity. After a few more short runs I hoisted a massive 30 inch walleye into the boat with my happy client yelling,

"This is the largest fish I have ever caught!"

To be honest, I did not expect to catch anything out of the hole. I thought to myself maybe that by using the larger minnow, he might stick a northern pike and we would avoid getting skunked. Although it was one of the largest walleyes I have ever boated, due to the nasty weather, I did not bring along my camera bag. This was before the digital age when you could stuff a camera in your pocket. I guess if you are only going to catch one walleye in a day, it might as well be a 30 incher.

Deep holes downstream from dams are notorious for holding both pre-spawn and post spawn walleyes. Pre-spawn walleyes can be very active and with the exception of a drop in the water temperature they can be counted on for consistent action. While there is no such thing as a sure thing, fishing the first deep hole downstream from the dam will hold walleyes from late winter through summer. In fact, I have fished several holes on my home river that hold big walleyes throughout the entire open water period.

The key is to find the first hole downstream and not

the second or third. The hole creates both a staging area for spawning bound walleyes and a resting place for them to avoid the current after spawning. The only problem I have when fishing the honey hole is in deciding when to fish it; not what period but what time of day. When I am guiding I never like to make my first stop the honey hole. I like to get a read on my clients and get some sense of their ability and the bite of the day. So we usually start out fishing secondary areas first. Additionally, if the fishing is good I don't have to reveal my honey hole to my clients.

The Herrilds' with walleyes from the Honey Hole

Most of the time by the time I get to a downstream hole it is mid-morning or even afternoon. Contrary to the belief of many walleye anglers you don't have to be on the river at sun up, you just need to know where walleyes are going to be at mid-day. Not only do you know where to fish at mid-day but you need to know where the walleyes will bite at mid-day. The thing about a downstream hole is that walleyes tend to be most active at mid-day. Remember that the walleyes are on the back side of a lip out of the current. The increased light penetration later in the day sparks some movement and many times this movement indirectly results in walleyes going on the feed.

Due to the current, vertical jigging is tough for most anglers unless your boat is rigged with an overpowering trolling motor. I rely on anchoring over the hole since it allows me to fish the entire hole effectively. On overcast days I look for walleyes to be pushed tight to the lip or upstream edge of the hole, so it is important to position your boat as closely to the lip as possible. As I stated earlier, on sunny days the walleyes are mobile so positioning right over the hole is best. If you are dealing with overcast skies early in the day and clearing skies later in the day, you can expect the walleye activity to intensify as the day progresses.

The time of day I fish a downstream hole will dictate the type of presentation that I use. Early in the day I rely on a plain jighead with a minnow, or I dead stick a live shiner on a plain hook with a split shot clinched about a foot above the hook. I try to get out of the current and vertical jig the minnow from one to three feet above the bottom. If the current is not too swift, you can use a slip bobber. When you feel a strike, drop your rod tip a few inches below the water and when you feel the weight of the walleye make a slow steady upward sweep. This is the same rig that I have been catching walleyes with for 30 years, and it is still effective to this day.

As the day progresses and the bite picks up, my method still works but a jig and minnow or a jig and curly tail grub tipped with a minnow becomes more effective. When using the jig I both vertical jig and cast and retrieve the jig. If you are fishing with a partner, one angler should use a different presentation. Unless one angler starts lighting the river on fire, continue to use both presentations if a few fish are caught. This way you will cover more water and catch both the active and neutral walleyes. A floating crankbait on a slip sinker rig is also effective. However, if the bite slows down with the jig I revert back to my old reliable method.

Post spawn walleyes will stack up in these holes but fishing for them can be very difficult unless you are deal-ing with stable weather and warming water tempera-tures. Most often during the post spawn, walleye will stack up in the hole only to avoid the current; feeding is not at the top of their agenda. However, just as during the pre-spawn the warm sun can motivate a big walleye. The sun can warm the water a degree or two pushing them to move, so that a properly placed river shiner will be tough to pass up. During the post spawn don't expect much in a downstream hole unless you are in a warming trend.

Most walleye anglers tend to focus on large areas or areas with abrupt changes such as a hole downstream from a dam, thinking that they will find a big load of fish. While it is a good practice to look for high concentrations of walleyes, don't overlook small areas. These areas can be a small current break with downed wood, a transition from rock to sand, or a submerged wood that breaks the current. There have been many days while guiding under the most adverse conditions where these small areas have been my ace in the hole, producing walleyes when all else seemed to fail.

When walleye are in pre-spawn a slight current break with downed wood is my go to area. A current break with downed wood can hold a load of walleyes when the water temperature drops a few degrees and walleyes are pushed out of the spawning mode. They seem to find comfort in wood as the water temperature drops and the more wood the better, as I found out while fishing with two bass fishermen one spring.

My fishing partners for the day had fished with me several times in the summer for river smallmouth but they both like to catch the occasional walleye, especially in spring when the smallmouth season was closed. We met one April morning and bought a generous supply of fathead and shiner minnows. On the ride to the landing I explained that the water temperature had dropped a couple of degrees and we would have to rely on finesse presentations and perhaps a little luck. In the back of my mind I tried to figure out what is harder, teaching a wall-eye fisherman how to bass fish or teaching a bass fisher-man how to fish for walleyes.

After I launched the boat we headed up river towards a dam and I positioned the boat over a hole on the back side of a rock ledge. The current was moderate and I was able to hold over the hole with my trolling motor allowing us to vertical jig the hole. Now keep in mind I was with 2 bass fishermen who had never previously vertical jigged for walleye. It took a while for them to understand that we were not supposed to cast and retrieve the bait but instead vertically jig the jig and minnow off the bottom and let it drop back down.

I said sarcastically, "This is easy, all you need to do is

find the right jig weight and keep the jig vertical and when you feel a strike set the hook." They just looked at me and laughed.

They kind of mastered the vertical jigging technique, keeping the line as vertical as possible, but even though I had marked lots of fish in the hole, we could not connect with a walleye. Truthfully, they had lots of pickups but due to the brisk wind, I had all I could do to control the boat and was unable to fish. Finally one of the guys said he had a strike and reared back like he was setting the hook of a plastic worm on a 10 pound largemouth bass. Needless to say he got the jig back minus the minnow and the walleye. Within the next few minutes the other guy had a strike, and, repeating his partner's hookset, the results were the same.

I knew it was time for me to concentrate on my vertical jigging in hopes to detect a strike. As I detected a strike I told my partners to watch as I lifted my rod in a hard sweep and set the hook on a 17 inch walleye. After a few missed hooksets they finally got the knack. The problem was that by the time they got the feel for vertical jigging the walleye bite was over.

We tried several other holes and structure where the locator showed many walleyes but the drop in water temperature had made for a tough bite. While we had caught a few walleyes, my partners knew they had missed several fish and for their sake I still hoped that we could run into a few more before we ended the day. I told them we needed to find some new cover and some walleyes that were a bit more aggressive.

I moved to a favorite area of mine which was a series of downed trees on a steep shoreline. As I slowed down the boat one of the guys pointed out that we had fished this wood together the past summer with topwater baits and we had caught a ton of smallmouth. I replied, "Yes, this is the place, but there are walleyes here right now!"

I put down the trolling motor and gave the guys some lighter jigs with thin wire weed guards instructing them to cast tight to the wood without casting into the wood. If walleyes were present I assured them that they would be tight to the wood due to the drop in water temperature. One of the guys caught a 17 inch male walleye on the third cast and within a few minutes the other guy scored with a comparable walleye. The action continued and we boated 24 walleyes from the wood with the largest one measuring 25 inches. Mixed in with the walleyes were four nice bonus smallmouth bass.

Typical River Walleye

Hard Baits

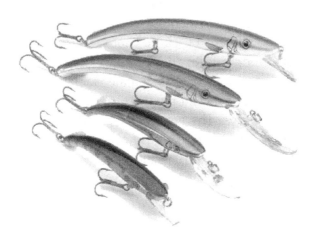

   While plastics work great, when the bite is tough, even the pros have trouble sticking walleyes. The new biodegradable baits offer another option. These baits look and feel like plastic, but are scented, and being biodegradable they won't scar the environment. A few of these baits will dispense scent through the water like a blood trail, telling fish that it is really food and expanding the strike zone. Biodegradable minnows come in 2 ½", 3"and 4" sizes as well as several color combinations. You can rig these minnows on a jighead, on a live bait hook or spinner rig using the same presentation you would use with a live minnow. A six foot six or seven foot medium or medium light action rod works best for these presentations. I spool my reels with a Hybrid monofilament/fluorocarbon line in six or eight pound test. The hybrid line is abrasion resistant, has limited memory and has good sensitivity along with not absorbing water, which allows the crankbait to run to a maximum depth.

Crankbaits come in a variety of colors, shapes and sizes and will catch walleyes. One of my all time favorite walleye crankbaits is the Yo-Zuri Crystal Minnow. The brilliant holographic laser tape finish of the Crystal Minnow reflects all subsurface light and gives a walleye a target even in murky water. The animated over-sized 3D eyes and raised molded gill plate add to the realistic appearance. A few of my favorite colors include orange/yellow, black/silver, chartreuse/silver and silver/bronze.

Shore fishing can be extremely productive and is often overlooked. Casting a Crystal Minnow or Crank'n Shad will often out produce live bait fishermen. A crankbait can be worked over rocks and easily retrieved along a current break, not to mention the fact that a crankbait will enable you to cover water more effectively.

Spring river walleye fishing need not be hit and miss. No, you don't have to sit home and wait for somebody to tell you that the walleyes are running. Once the ice leaves the river you need not be far behind. Be versatile in both the locations in which you are looking for walleyes and in your presentation.

Chapter Three
Above The Dam

As stated in the previous chapter, it is hard to beat spring walleye fishing on a river below a dam. Up here in the North Country, not only is spring your first chance at open water, it can also be very productive. However, there are also excellent opportunities *above* the dam. Most of this action gets underway after the peak run on the river is on the downswing. Nevertheless, if you put in your time rewards can abound.

Although walleyes will act like walleyes regardless of

what type of water they populate, they will take on a completely different personality on various types of water. The walleye angler that understands the uniqueness of each individual type of water and how walleyes react to these differences will put more fish in the boat. Simply put, if you use the same tactics that you used while fishing moving water, you could get skunked while fishing above the dam. That is not to say that you need to avoid fishing reservoirs or natural lakes in spring, you just need to refine your presentations.

In my 30 years of on the water experience I have spent countless days fishing reservoirs for walleyes and have had good days and, yes, many slow days as well. Walleye anglers know that you can be fishing the best walleye water in North America and still come up short. This can be caused by the weather patterns, water levels, a drop in water temperature, or let's face it, fisherman incompetence. Sure there are many days where walleyes just have a case of lock jaw, but many times the angler's poor success rate can be attributed to their presentation, rather than being on the wrong water at the wrong time.

Most of my fishing for reservoir walleyes has been in the upper Midwest. While I have fished for both largemouth bass and smallmouth bass on reservoirs in the southern Midwest and the Mid-South, I just never got around to pursuing walleyes in these reservoirs. I have caught a few walleyes while bass fishing but never figured out if they were just incidental catches or if the reservoirs I was fishing had fishable walleye populations.

Southern reservoirs are much larger than their northern counterparts and much more diverse. Keep in mind when I say Southern waters, I am referring to anything south of the Great Lakes. Some southern reservoirs contain clear water with visibility down to 20 plus feet, while others look like chocolate milk. Along with the variations in water clarity, anglers are also faced with the massive size of most southern reservoirs. The large size of the reservoir can overwhelm an angler who is familiar with the reservoir, let alone a first time angler.

Where ever walleyes are found, one thing is for certain is they have to eat. Knowing the preferred walleye forage on a body of water is always the key in locating and catching walleyes. Northern reservoirs usually have an abundant forage base while southern reservoirs tend to have a restricted forage base. Since bass are the dominant predators in most southern reservoirs, walleyes will take a back seat to the bass polulations. Feeding times are tough to pattern and walleyes can be tough to locate. However, since walleyes receive less fishing pressure, a seasoned walleye angler can do well.

Even an old bass fisherman like me can catch a load of walleyes on southern reservoirs by refining your presentation, once you catch that initial walleye.

Several years ago I was fishing for largemouth bass on a medium-sized Kansas reservoir in late March. The reservoir was a power plant lake just a few miles west of the Missouri Line with murky water and very limited visibility. It was a Flatland Reservoir with almost no bottom structure and locating the river channel was like finding a needle in a haystack. The reservoir was known primarily for largemouth bass but it has a good striper population and walleyes were listed as present. My brother Scott, who was living south of Kansas City at the time, had said that he had caught an occasional walleye and that he had never seen anyone fishing specifically for them.

One April day we were catching lots of largemouth bass on crankbaits while fishing a rip rap shoreline where the bass were feeding on shad. The shad were suspended and the bass were chasing them big time. We were using typical bass style crankbaits like Rat-L-Traps and Bombers. Color did not seem to matter since we were catching the bass on Fire/Tiger, blue/silver and black/shad. It was one of those days when you could not make a bad cast or pick the wrong color.

We continued to catch lots of bass until we found ourselves dodging crankbaits that were falling inches from out boat. Seems like these fisherman down here were just like fisherman back home, in that they did not depend on their locators to find bass, they just watched other anglers. Instead of fighting the circus, we decided to back off and fall behind the school of shad. We had already caught plenty of quality bass, so I really did not care if we caught anymore, I was just concerned for our safety and I told Scott that there had to be more fish somewhere in the lake.

Knowing that the bass were feeding on shad, we were looking for more schools of shad hoping to connect with more bass. We finally located two schools of baitfish, with one suspending 10 feet above the other. Below the deeper cloud of baitfish were several large fish. With the deeper school of shad suspending at 20 feet, we knew fishing crankbaits might be tough, but as active as the bass we had caught had been, we figured we could catch them, or at least give them a serious effort.

I had plenty of jigs and grubs in my bag of tricks and we started making casts, letting the jigheads fall to the desired depths. The first dozen or so casts yielded no fish and we figured that these bass were not on the feed like the others. Finally, I rigged a shad body bait on my lead head jig and let it drop to about 20-25 feet. We were positioned right over the school of baitfish and predator fish and I began to vertical jig and I told Scott that this was just like back home on the river.

It did not take long and I felt a strike and set the hook. I told my brother that the fish had plenty of weight but that it wasn't fighting very hard. All the fish wanted to do was dive to deep water. I was eventually able to pull the fish up to the boat and told Scott that this was no bass but a big walleye. The walleye measured 24 inches and was released back into the reservoir. We caught eight more walleye between 24 and 27 inches and, of course, drew a crowd. However, they did not stick around once they figured out we were catching walleyes and not bass.

The only problem we had is that after catching walleye we would have liked to have taken home a meal. However, we realized that these big walleyes were not that abundant on that reservoir and that keeping them would not have been good. We did not know if walleyes spawned in the reservoir, or if they relied on stocking. I believe the reservoir had a minimum size of 18 inches, but we could not find a walleye under 24 inches. I told Scott that if we would have known we would be looking for smaller eating sized walleyes we could have brought a few dozen nightcrawlers along.

The lesson learned here was that although walleyes were feeding on shad like the bass, they were suspending deeper in the water column. This is a typical situation that anglers will encounter when walleye fishing regardless of their destination. On any water where walleyes are not the dominant predator fish they will follow the food chain but relate to the deeper water. Even though we were catching big walleyes, they were no match for the large school of largemouth bass. If walleyes were the dominant predator in the reservoir they would have been feeding on both the shallow and deep shad and they also would have aggressively hit our crankbaits.

My brother has long since moved away and I know that

I will never fish that reservoir again. It is typical of many in the lower Midwest and Mid-South. The walleye population may not have been overly large, but nevertheless, quality walleyes were present. Even though the numbers might have been low, the locals had no apparent interest in catching them. Who knows, either those people were sitting on a prime walleye fishery or we just might have caught a few stragglers.

While each northern reservoir, or "flowage" as they are called in my home state of Wisconsin, will have its own unique personality, they typically have more in common than they are different. Although there are exceptions, a typical northern reservoir usually has stained water, a distinct river channel, ample structure and a variety of forage. Walleyes share their environment with both largemouth and smallmouth bass like their Southern counterparts but also share the water with northern pike and muskies. Even though more predators are present, walleyes are easier to pattern due to the diverse structure and forage.

The one big plus factor up north, is that anglers have more reservoirs from which to choose. Some reservoirs are small, covering only a few hundred acres, while others can cover several thousand acres. The variety of the size of the reservoir will dictate what time of year they are likely to be the most productive. It is not a hit or miss situation, but rather putting the odds in your favor by picking the right water.

Keep in mind that reservoirs are still part of a river system. Some reservoirs will have one main tributary feeding it while others can have one main river and a few smaller feeder streams. On occasion you will find a reservoir that has more than one major tributary forming the reservoir. Numerous tributaries entering the reservoir might mean a higher walleye population since more suitable spawning is available. However, it can also mean that walleye can scatter in a variety of locations. One year they can be stacked in one location and the next year they'll be scattered over several areas.

Water levels will often dictate what route walleyes take when spawning. During high water years walleyes can migrate far upstream and congregate below waterfalls, rapids or dams. Under periods of low water walleyes may not be able to swim upstream to suitable spawning areas and most of the spawning will take place in the reservoir. During any given year most reservoirs will see both spawning migrations upriver and spawning in the reservoir. Remember to keep in mind that each reservoir is different and nothing is set in stone.

One reservoir I have fished extensively over the past 30 some years is High Falls Flowage located in Northeast Wisconsin. High Falls is a 1,800 acre reservoir with a maximum depth of 50 feet. It has steep rock shorelines with many shoreline points and off shore humps making it a structure fisherman's paradise. High Falls can be broken into two distinctly different basins, the deeper and wider southern portion and the shallower narrow northern portion. The southern portion resembles a natural lake and the northern portion resembles a river, giving walleyes plenty of places to call home.

While I have done well on High Falls Flowage, it can be a very unpredictable place to fish for walleyes due to the abundant structure. The secret to success is in knowing walleye location during the spawn while also recognizing the amount of water flowing through the reservoir. Over the years I have watched the same people fish the same areas on the reservoir. One year they caught lots of walleyes and the next year they would get skunked. Although the water level of the reservoir was the same each year, the volume of water flowing through the reservoir caused walleyes to spawn in a different location.

In years when there is a high volume of water moving through the flowage, walleyes will spawn and quickly move back downstream into the reservoir. If you do not hit it just right, with the water temperature holding around 41-45 degrees, you will miss out on the action. Spawning can be over in a matter of a few days. Not only does the high water make for a quick spawn, but the spawn is tough on female walleyes. Being stressed out due to the spawn, female walleyes will avoid the current and hold tight to structure. Unfortunately, when holding tight to cover, these walleye are not easy to pick up, even with good electronics. Add the fact that the high water level will keep the water temperature from rising and anglers can experience a tough bite.

There have been times when fishing during high water when my clients and I have practically had to knock the walleye on the head in order to get their attention. During pre-spawn, walleyes will hold on the deep edge of the current break behind rocks, or even wood, and wait until the water temperature climbs over 42 degrees. Even if you find them, they might not chase a bait more than a few inches. They move up to spawn and are out of there. This can be a guide's worst scenario, unless you hit it just right. If you hit it just right, your clients think you can walk on water, but if you miss the spawn, it can be a guide's nightmare.

One day several years ago, I hit it just right and we could have loaded the boat with walleyes. Not only were we hit with a large volume of water flowing through the reservoir but a cold front had dropped the water temperature down to 40 degrees. Any time you have a drop in the water temperature just before spawning, feeding is the last thing walleyes are concerned about. Needless to say, I did not expect our day to be very productive.

I chose to start fishing a few shoreline points on the southern end of the flowage. The points were out of the main force of the wind and current would be nonexistent. If walleyes were present, it was usually a no brainer to boat a couple of legal walleyes. The fish turned out to be on the deep edge of the first point that we fished, but they had lock jaw and refused everything we threw at them. The only active fish was a 20 inch northern pike that nailed a fathead minnow tipped on a 1/16 orange leadhead jig. After the pike it was time to move onto the next point.

The locator showed walleyes holding on the deep edge of the point but there were a couple of fish suspended about two feet off the bottom. Since the fish were suspended a few feet off the bottom, I told my clients that there was a good chance that these fish would be slightly more aggressive. My clients made a couple of casts and each of them had a fish. Unfortunately the fish turned out to be northern pike that were clones of the one we had caught on the last point. Just before were about to move, one of my clients caught a 14 inch walleye. We decided to hang around but after 20 minutes of no fish we decided to make a move. I told my clients that we were going to make a major move and head into the river.

As I drove to the northern end of High Falls where the Peshtigo River entered the reservoir, I was trying to figure out where the walleyes would be. Would they be stacked in the deep hole at the river mouth, the logjam at the edge of the creek channel or holding on the edge of the deep rocks below the big boulder in the middle of the river. Hopefully, I would find walleyes in one of the locations and salvage the day.

The cold front brought with it a brisk 25 MHP northwest wind that I knew would be blowing right down the pipe.

Even in the narrow river, it would be tricky to avoid the full force of the wind and stay on the fish. Due to the current, positioning the boat with my electric trolling motor was out of the question. The only option was to try to anchor over the walleyes; all I had to do was find some, which under the conditions could be next to impossible. While my clients were well aware of the fact that the conditions were not good for catching a limit of walleyes, they also knew they were in good hands.

Our first stop was the deep hole at the mouth of the river that to this day seems to always hold a few walleyes. The river narrows and drops from eight feet to twenty two feet. The steep rock ledge was probably a water fall before the dam was built in 1910. Besides catching lots of walleyes from this hole, I often reminisce as to how majestic the spot must have been before the dam was built. Then again if the dam was not built I would not be fishing for walleyes out of a boat. The spot was probably a classic brook trout spot, one of many for which the Peshtigo River was famous.

Although this spot always holds a few walleyes, catching them is a different story. It was one of those places that if the locator marked fish they were probably walleyes, but you had about a sixty percent chance of catching them. As I expected, the hole was full of walleyes and they were everywhere. Some were holding tight to the bottom while others were suspended one to two feet from the bottom. I pointed to my locator and my clients lit up like a Christmas tree; we all figured that we were in business. Actually, I figured that we would catch a few limits in no time, which could make for a short day. The air temperature was drop-ping and the wind velocity was on the rise.

Well, so much for luck. After making several casts without a bite, my clients now had a look of despair. They wondered out loud if their lack of success was due to their poor fishing ability and encouraged me to start making a few casts. While I do fish with my clients, I always let them make the first few casts, especially in an area where I know fish are present. Knowing the bite was tough, I tied on a 1/8 ounce chartreuse leadhead jig and tipped it with a large fathead minnow. We had shiners but the smaller fathead minnow will often do the trick under adverse conditions.

Just as I had suspected, my clients lack of success was not their fault, it was a result of the deplorable conditions with which we were dealing. After several casts and several different color jigs, I knew that this was not the place. What had happened was the hole was so full of walleyes that they were stacked up like cordwood and there was no room for any more walleye on the bottom. I told them that we could stay in this hole the rest of the day and watch the locator and not catch any fish. Instead they agreed that it was time for a change.

The next spot was on the edge of a creek channel. I told my clients that I had occasionally caught a few walleyes on the edge of the channel but that the spot was not high on my priority list. I was hoping to catch a couple of walleyes just to break the ice and get a walleye in the livewell. By now we would all be happy to see a 15 inch walleye no matter who caught it.

As I slowed the boat I scanned the log jam on the edge of the slough searching for any signs of life. Needless to say, I found nothing except what appeared to be floating debris pushed over the wood from the swift current. I knew that there could be walleyes under the debris hunkered down under the wood, but also knew that if they were there they would not jump on our jigs. If the walleye in the hole wouldn't cooperate you wouldn't expect these wood walleye to be on the feed.

I don't know why, other than to call it my sixth sense,

but I decided to fish the spot anyway. Using my anchor I positioned the boat so it was right over the wood. My clients began vertical jigging over the top of the wood and casting and retrieving a jig and minnow along the deep and shallow edge of the wood. Finally, one of my clients con-nected with a 16 inch walleye. I did not know if we were in business or if it was the old adage that even a blind squirrel will find an acorn every once in a while. Anyway, we were technically not skunked for the day.

We made a few more casts to no avail and suddenly the anchor rope broke loose. I just shook my head thinking that we finally found an active walleye and now we were on the move whether we liked it or not. However, as suddenly as the boat stared to move it came to an abrupt halt and I nearly fell off the front deck of the boat. I heard my client in the back of the boat yell but was almost afraid to look at him for fear that he had lost his balance and had gone for an unexpected swim. What I saw instead was an anxious angler with a big smile and a bent rod; just what a guide likes to see.

I jumped to the back of the boat picking up the landing net on the way and lifted a 24 inch walleye into the boat. It was a female walleye and her belly was full of eggs. The fish was released and all three of us were quick to get a rod into the river. Within a matter of a few seconds the same guy hooked another nice walleye which I again hoisted into the boat. This one was bigger, measuring 28 inches. This time I knew we were in business.

About the time we released the walleye the other guy connected and I ran to the front of the boat and landed a 19 inch walleye, which was put into the livewell. The action continued and I kept netting walleyes. The guy in the front of the boat caught a few more 19 inch walleyes and the guy in the back of the boat caught several walleyes over 24 inches. They switched places and the back of the boat kept producing lunkers and the front of the boat kept producing eaters. It was the perfect scenario for a walleye angler. I don't recall the actual number of walleye we caught, but I do know that each client caught his 5 walleye limit and they each boated a walleye over 28 inches.

Walleyes from the woodpile

The lesson learned here is that sometimes walleyes need a bit of persuasion. While a few sticks of dynamite might have shaken up the wood pile, I don't think the DNR would have given me a permit. However, a well placed anchor can also shake up a wood pile. We tried to retrieve the anchor out of the wood pile, but considering the results, I gladly sacrificed the anchor to the walleye gods.

Granted, this was a few years back and electronics have come a long way, but it is interesting how we caught fish where we did not mark them with the locator. We marked tons of walleyes in the hole in the mouth of the river and caught nothing. This just goes to show that you can't rely only on your electronics. If a spot has held fish for you in the past, give the spot a shot, even if you don't mark fish on your electronics. Take care not to make the mistake of fishing there all day simply because you caught a load of walleyes there back in 1989. I have returned to that spot many times and have never even come close to the success we had that May Day.

Those same clients have fished with me occasionally for smallmouth bass, and on each trip we reminisce about the great day we had walleye fishing on High Falls. I never did let them know that it was an accident and that if that anchor rope had not slipped, we might have gotten skunked. Some things a guide just has to keep to himself.

Generally the best walleye fishing on High Falls occurs in years when a low volume of water is flowing through the reservoir. At that time walleyes will move out of the reservoir and enter the river to spawn. Due to the low water they are unable to make a long migration. Actual spawning will take place on the edge of sloughs, creeks, or shoreline current breaks. These can be the same areas in which they spawned under high water, except they won't spawn tight to the shoreline. Although they are deeper, the slower current will have a tendency to concentrate walleyes both before and after spawning. With walleyes staying in the area for a longer period of time, anglers have an opportunity to be on fish for a longer period of time as well. This is unlike high water when you have to hit the conditions and the walleyes just right to be successful, leaving the angler with little room for error.

Not all walleyes will migrate upstream to spawn if suitable spawning habitat is present in the reservoir. During some years, for whatever the reason, the bulk of the walleyes can remain in the reservoir to spawn on shoreline points and gravel and rock shorelines. This usually happens in years when the water is slow to warm and these slower water warming conditions mean that walleye spawning will take place for an extended time period.

Small reservoirs can have phenomenal walleye populations and anglers who tap into these fisheries can have consistent action for years on end. The only problem that can arise is that small reservoirs are prone to overharvest. Many smaller reservoirs will go through peaks and valleys with stable walleye populations being rare. The more remote the reservoir is, the lighter the fishing pressure. The lighter the fishing pressure, the higher the odds for a good walleye population.

Walleyes from a small reservoir

One of my favorite small reservoirs covers just 140 acres and it has only one major inlet. The inlet is a trout stream which usually has high water in spring. Walleyes will travel about four miles to spawn below a water fall. While there are a few rock and gravel areas throughout the reservoir none of it seems to be suitable for walleye spawning. I estimate that well over 90 percent of the walleyes in the reservoir would spawn below the waterfall. With 90 percent of the walleye population spawning in a small area, it is easy to see why the fishing is incredible.

The fishing pattern is easy, locate a current break near the waterfall, flip a jig and minnow and wait for a strike. When walleyes are stacked up like cord wood in a small area, they tend to cooperate well. You will have to experiment with the size of the jig so that you can crawl it along the bottom, picking up as few snags as possible. A favorite tactic of mine is to cast the jig on the edge of the current and let it drift into the slack water. Once your jig drifts into the slack water, reel up the slack line and give the jig a few short pops. After the short pops, watch the line for movement and then set the hook. When setting the hook use a steady upward swing.

Jig color can be important but in general, orange and chartreuse work best in the stained river water. If the bite is hot, you might not even need minnows. Three and four inch twister tails in white, yellow, orange and chartreuse will often out produce minnows. Not only does the twister tail add color but the added vibration triggers savage strikes. There have been many times when I thought it was a northern pike hitting my jig. Occasionally the bite can be light, particularly if walleyes have just completed spawning. If you are dealing with a light bite, try a shiner minnow on an Aberdeen hook and dead stick it off the side of the boat.

Small reservoirs do have pronounced shoreline points

and humps that attract loads of spawning walleyes. On most reservoirs, the size of the spawning area will dictate the number of walleyes that will use the structure for spawning. With prime spawning structure being limited, most walleye spawning will take place in only one or two areas.

A small reservoir can be very difficult to fish for spring walleye if walleye spawning is scattered throughout the reservoir. This usually occurs when the feeder creeks or river entering the reservoir are not suitable for walleye spawning. It is common for a small reservoir to contain isolated spawning areas that are too small to attract large numbers of walleyes. A small gravel shoreline, a rocky point or an off shore hump can hold a few walleye. These isolated spawning areas are tough to locate and even when they are found, due to the low density of walleyes, it will take an educated eye to spot them on a locator. I have watched many anglers pass up a good spot just because they did not mark any walleyes on their locator.

nstead of looking for walleyes, I look for transition areas from rock/gravel to wood. Walleyes will spawn on the rock and gravel but the areas are too small to hold them prior to and after spawning. During the pre-spawn big females hold tight to the wood regardless of the weather conditions. Wood acts as a staging area until the water temp. reaches the mid forties and the eggs are ripe. So when the water temperature is between 40-43 degrees use your electronics to search for wood and not actual walleyes.

If the wood is shallower than 15 feet, I position my boat with my electric trolling motor and vertical jig in the manor explained in chapter one. When the wood is deeper than 15 feet I prefer to use the anchor to position the boat over the wood. When anchored I will both vertical jig and cast and retrieve a jig and minnow. Weedless jigs will aid in avoiding the snags, but they will not eliminate them altogether. I have yet to see a totally weedless jig that can be fished around submerged wood. The bite can be light and you might have trouble distinguishing a bite from a snag, but that's walleye fishing.

Another deadly tactic is to rig a minnow under a slip bobber. Set one slip bobber about one foot above the bottom close to the stump. Next, set another slip bobber a few inches over the stump or wood pile. The minnow suspended over the stump is the real teaser and can attract the largest walleye of the day. I learned this tactic years ago when fishing for crappie. One of my clients tied into an eight pound walleye while fishing a crappie minnow on four pound test line.

Wood has produced many catches of post spawn walleye even under deplorable conditions. On small reservoirs walleye tend to move as little as possible after spawning. With wood usually being the first available structure they encounter after spawning, wood can hold the mother lode. Female post spawn walleyes in particular have been known to crawl under a big submerged stump. A slip bobber and minnow is tailor made for this situation. If you are after a big walleye you will need to put in your time.

The bigger the reservoir does not mean the better the walleye fishing. Larger reservoirs can have a healthy walleye population but the ratio of walleyes to acre of water may not be all that high. Walleyes can scatter throughout the reservoir as they feed on a variety of different types of forage. On large reservoirs the forage base can vary from year to year making fish tough to pattern. The Michigamme Reservoir in Michigan's Upper Peninsula fits into this category. I have fished it from time to time over the years and I have had my good days and bad days. It is one of those places that if you hit it just right, the fishing can be unbeliev-able.

The Michigamme Reservoir is a large reservoir fed by the Michigamme River, Fence River, Margeson River and Deer River. There were five natural lakes in the main basin prior to the creation of the reservoir. Due to the fluctuating water levels, it is hard to put a handle on the actual size of the reservoir but it averages around 7,000 surface acres. Walleyes are a big part of the fishery but northern pike, musky, smallmouth bass and largemouth bass are also present.

In spring, all of the rivers entering the reservoir see spawning walleyes. The Fence River and the Michigamme River, which enter the reservoir on the northwest, are the primary spawning areas, at least most of the time. It is like the walleyes are here today and gone tomorrow; not a good place for a fishing guide to take a client.

However, if you do hit it right the client will think you walk on water. I had been telling a friend of mine about the Michigamme Reservoir for a few years and promised him that we would spend a day on the reservoir. He was a reliable friend and I knew his lips would be sealed so if we did get into a load of walleyes the rest of the county would not know about it.

The weather was stable, and the water temperature was on the rise. As I launched my boat I was surprised to see that the water temperature was 58 degrees and I told my partner that it looked like the walleyes had completed spawning and that they should be hungry. I wasn't just trying to inflate our hopes of success, I really felt confident that day.

Since I knew that the walleyes had completed spawning and the weather had been stable, I knew if we found forage we would find feeding walleyes. Weeds are limited in the reservoir but I knew of one cabbage bed that I stumbled on a few years ago. If I could find that cabbage bed I knew it would be filled with baitfish and feeding walleyes.

Any reservoir where the water level fluctuates will usually see limited weedgrowth. Over the years I have noticed that even though the amount of weedgrowth will vary the weeds will grow in the same place annually. The only problem was that this was in the Stone Age, prior to the GPS and I had to rely on my sixth sense to find the honey hole. I also knew that if I did not find this spot it might have taken half the day to locate let alone figure out a pattern to catch walleyes.

Sometimes I think that anglers rely too much on electronic gadgets to do their work for them. I fish with a lot of younger people who are good anglers but if you take away their electronics they are lost. To this day, I feel that one of the reasons I do catch a lot of fish is that I rely on my experience and not on gadgets. Not that a locator hasn't saved the day many a time, but if an angler can learn to get a feel for the water he will catch more fish.

After carefully navigating through a series of rock humps, I approached a flat bottom area well downstream from where one of the rivers entered the reservoir. On the edge of the flat there was a steep breakline dropping to 20 feet. I did use my electronics to see if there were any walleyes on the break but nobody was home. I told my partner that we were going to fish the flat. Most walleye anglers would not have given the area a second glance but this flat is where we would hopefully locate fresh weeds.

We were in Michigan so we were able to troll, which is illegal back home in Northern Wisconsin. We rigged up spinner rigs tipped with nightcrawlers and minnows and slowly backtrolled in 10 feet of water. As I zigzagged across the flat hoping to find weeds and walleyes, after 45 minutes it did not look promising.

Suddenly my partner yelled, "Fish On." Walleyes are not known for their fighting ability so it did not take long to flip an 18 inch walleye into the boat. Besides admiring the nice eating sized walleye, I told my partner to look at the stalk of fresh cabbage weed in the net. We continued to backtroll right in the sparse weeds and continued to catch walleyes. No big walleye but plenty of fish for a meal. We caught and released several walleyes between 14 and 20 inches. These were probably all male walleyes which were feeding on shiners which in turn were feeding on perch fry that had hatched two or three weeks earlier. I told my partner that we found the food chain and that we were at the top of it.

Backtrolling caught these weed walleyes

We had a good day on the water and caught lots of weed related walleyes. However, we had hit everything just right. If the water temperature had been colder and a cold front had passed, I am almost certain the results would have been very different. The lesson learned here is that larger complex reservoirs have plenty to offer including big walleyes, but the fishing is tough to pattern and can confuse even the most seasoned angler. As you can see, if I had to choose between a small and large reservoir for spring walleyes, the small reservoir gets the nod.

When fishing reservoirs one question that has puzzled me for years is the finesse presentations necessary to catch reservoir walleye. While I have caught many walleyes on finesse presentations, I have caught equally as many walleyes by triggering a strike with spinners or crankbaits. While nothing is set in stone, by following the basics, you will put more fish in the boat.

Jigs

A light 1/16 ounce or 1/8 ounce jig and fathead minnow is deadly when fishing in shallow stained water. One problem that can arise when using light jigs is finding one with an oversized hook. The oversized hook will allow you to tip the jig with a smaller minnow. Use a slow steady retrieve with your jig. A stop and retrieve presentation will often produce the most walleyes.

Due to the stained water, bright fluorescent colored jigs work the best. You will find that each reservoir might have a preferred color but the hot color can change from day to day or throughout the day.

The water in shallow reservoirs tends to be darker and finesse presentations are only necessary after a cold front or drop in water temperature. After a cold front use lighter line and crawl your jig as slowly as possible. Quite often, no retrieve is the best retrieve.

Line

Six or eight pound test will usually get the job done on reservoirs. Reservoirs contain stumps, rock and rubble which are not friendly to four pound test. Heavier ten pound test might not spook walleyes in stained water but the heavier line will not sink as fast as lighter line. I have observed that many times a client fishing with ten pound test line will catch fewer fish than a client using six or eight pound test line. The lighter line gets to the bottom faster and stays in the strike zone longer on the retrieve.

Crankbaits

While finesse presentations will catch lots of spring walleyes, don't get hung up on them. Crankbaits are walleye catchers and can quickly find active walleyes. I only know of a few reservoirs where crankbaits are not productive for walleyes. In spring, use minnow imitation crankbaits with a tight direct action.

Yes, each reservoir has its own personality and no two reservoirs can be fished the same. Learn the critical differences and you will up your odds of success.

Chapter Four
Early Season Walleye In Natural Lakes

Although catching fish is seldom easy, you can greatly increase your odds by fishing in the right place at the right time. On any given day you can fish on a lake and have a slow day, but sometimes if you would have just fished down the road a piece you could have caught more and bigger fish. Knowing when to fish a specific lake or section of river is what has kept me in the guide business for close to 30 years. While there is nothing cut in stone, by following a few simple patterns you can increase your odds. Far too many people spend most of their time fishing in the wrong place.

Walleye anglers in particular have the problem of falling into a rut. They fish the same lake each year for the season opener. It might be for convenience or they might feel comfortable on a lake they know, but if success is the objective, it is not a smart move. I fell into this rut too, and had it not been for guiding and trying to accommodate my clients, I would have missed out on some of the great fishing our area has to offer. This is not to say one lake is better than the other, just one lake is better on any given day.

If you have a late ice out, deep clear water lakes can produce monster walleyes on the spring opener. Big female walleye will move into spawning areas and anglers aware of these locations can cash in on a real Bonanza. Years back, I timed it just right on one clear water natural lake. Now, granted, the lake does not have the large walleye population it once had, but it still has trophy potential. I changed my plans at the last minute and it turned out to be one of the best opening days of walleye fishing that I had ever had.

I had originally planned to fish on High Falls Flowage, but it was a cold spring with unstable weather. My clients had fished with me previously and we had caught lots of walleyes; they had hopes of running into a big one. I explained to them that the walleyes had just completed spawning on High Falls. Now, as any walleye angler will tell you, fishing post- spawn walleyes after a cold front is a tough bite. Given effort, you might be able to catch a few eating sized fish just over the legal size, but hoping to catch a trophy walleye would be next to impossible.

However, I told them that if they were still anticipating a big walleye I had another lake on my list, the only stipulation being that their lips had to be sealed. Not that the lake was a secret lake hidden in the back country, but it was a tough lake to fish and few people had the patience to figure it out. I assured them that the walleyes would not jump in the boat, but that if we put in our time we had a shot at a few big walleyes. We picked up some golden shiners and headed west.

On the ride to the lake I explained to my clients that the lake had very clear water and limited structure. In summer and fall, the big walleyes would roam the deep water and, worse yet, suspend, making them tough to locate, let alone try to catch them. However, I pointed out that the ice had just gone off the lake and walleyes were in the pre-spawn which meant they were bunching up and feeding on spawning rainbow smelt. They were pumped and I hoped that I could deliver.

As we launched the boat, one of my clients commented that we were the only boat on the lake. I don't know if he was thinking it was a good thing since we had the lake to ourselves, or that the locals figured it was a poor fishing lake. I told him that was great since nobody would be in our way or watch us catch fish. Since they had fished with me before I knew they had confidence in the conditions.

As usual, the cold front brought along brisk northwest winds, but we were in luck since the small creek where the rainbow smelt were spawning was on the west end of the lake; once we arrived in the spot, the wind would not be an issue. Since we were out of the wind, I opted to use the electric trolling motor to move in for the kill. Whenever you are hunting big fish, regardless of the specie, it is important to be as stealthy as possible. Once big fish are spooked, the odds of them biting the rest of the day are slim.

Even though I expected the big walleyes to be in the vicinity of the creek feeding on rainbow smelt, I positioned the boat well out from the creek mouth. If we would have moved to shallow water we might have passed up the largest walleyes which were sitting in 25 feet of water.

Whenever you are fishing a prime area, always start fishing deep water first and then move shallow. Sure thing, my electronics showed several big arcs suspending five feet off the bottom and clouds of rainbow smelt.

My clients knew we were in business, but they also knew we had to catch them. As every angler knows, when predator fish are zeroed in on particular forage it can be feast or famine. We were in 25 feet of water and the walleyes were suspended five feet off the bottom; I stressed that we would have to put the bait right in front of them. While a walleye might rise up to hit bait, if the bait dropped below the walleye they would not respond to the offering.

I told them that I would position the boat right over the walleyes and we would vertical jig with blue jigs and shiner minnows. Although the walleyes were feeding on rainbow smelt, the shiner minnows were as close to the rainbow smelt as we could get. The blue jig would also aid in imitating the rainbow smelt since the rainbow smelt do have a blue/silver color pattern. When walleyes are feeding on any smelt of ciscoes, you can refrain from using the typical orange or chartreuse jigs.

Besides the jig and shiner, I also rigged a shiner on a slip bobber at 19 feet, which was one foot above where the walleyes were holding. I had faith in the jig and minnow presentation but I knew that the big fish of the day would come from the slip bobber rig. As I eased over the school of walleye both my clients felt resistance on the line, and since we were over open water, they were not snagged. However, neither guy was able to hook a walleye.

It remained slow for about a half hour then suddenly we had a strike on the slip bobber. After a quick conference the guy in the back of the boat grabbed the slip bobber rod and set the hook. In the clear water we could see the fish swimming up toward the boat and in a short time I netted a 28 inch walleye. Both my clients were looking for a 30 inch walleye so after a few pictures the 28 inch walleye was released. These guys know that if they had wanted to keep a boat load of big walleyes, I would not have taken them to this spot.

Walleyes eating rainbow smelt

After several walleyes in the 24-28 inch class one of my clients managed to connect with a hawg. The walleye measured exactly 30 inches and he decided to keep it to put on his wall. Keep in mind that this was prior to all the big walleyes being caught in the Great Lakes; 30 inch walleyes were hard to come buy regardless of where you fished. My clients had spent many years fishing in Canada and had never experienced walleye fishing like this.

We eventually moved to the edge of the creek and after a few casts one of my clients connected with a chunky 18 inch walleye which he proceeded to place into the live well and gave the 30 inch walleye some company. A few minutes later his partner also caught an eating sized walleye and within a short time they had plenty for a meal. The action continued the rest of the day and we were definitely in the right place at the right time.

That lake where we caught all those big walleyes was a medium sized natural lake that covered 1,500 acres. It was unique in that it has one prime area that attracts hungry walleyes. The overall walleye population was only fair but since they concentrate in a small area, spring fishing is excellent. By June walleyes will suspend and scatter throughout the lake as they chase the schools of smelt and ciscoes. Since trolling is illegal on most northern Wisconsin lakes, fishing can be very tough.

Just like small reservoirs, small natural lakes can also have great spring walleye fishing especially if they have a good forage base that will contribute to producing quality walleyes. A small lake can hold a good overall walleye population but the lack of sufficient forage to grow big walleyes can work against an angler looking for a trophy. Walleyes can exhibit a good growth rate but to attain a large size, they need the right forage. Most small lakes lack for sufficient smelt and ciscoes, and if the shiner and chub population is limited you won't find many large walleyes.

The majority of smaller walleye lakes are action lakes with most of the walleyes being just at or below the legal limit. With some sorting most anglers manage to usually get enough walleyes for a meal. The only problem that can arise is that fishing pressure can be high and catching legal walleyes can pose a challenge. If the fishing pressure is too high natural reproduction will not sustain a good fishery and stocking is necessary. Since walleye fisherman don't practice catch and release, they can be their own worst enemy. If walleye anglers would learn to practice selective harvest they would enhance their favorite lakes.

Fishing an action walleye lake in spring is seldom complicated, with the exception of a severe cold front, after which spawning walleyes are aggressive and relating to fresh weeds in search of a meal. The only problem is that weeds are sprouting up daily and walleyes can be anywhere. If trolling is allowed, backtrolling a spinner rig tipped with a crawler or minnow is the best method to find active walleyes. By using different weights and blades, you will be able to fish a variety of depths. Once you establish contact with walleyes, if the bite slows try experimenting with varying blade colors.

In water shallower than 15 feet, it is not necessary to keep the spinner rig in a vertical position. However, letting out too much line will allow too much slack in the line and you will not feel light bites. Most bites will be light and feel more like resistance as opposed to a strike. When you feel resistance on the line set the hook with a fast sweep of the rod.

When fishing in water deeper than 15 feet, it is important that you keep the spinner rig as vertical as possible. By keeping your line vertical, you will be able to detect the slightest resistance on the line. Make sure your sinker is heavy enough to get the spinner rig to the bottom. With the weight on the bottom, the spinner will spin freely with the movement of the boat. If the weight is off the bottom the spinner will not work properly, since the spinner will be fighting the weight and might not even spin. If the weight is too heavy, you will not spook walleyes, but the odds of getting snags are increased. Backtrolling with spinner rigs is much more than dragging a line behind the boat.

Forward trolling with crankbaits is also very effective,

particularly when it comes to catching larger walleyes. Walleyes are roaming the weeds feeding on baitfish and crankbaits are made to order in this situation. Choose your crankbait according to the depth of the weeds. Just like when backtrolling with spinner rigs, you will need to cover as much water as possible to locate a school of walleyes. Walleyes could be in the weeds, along the edges or fanning out along a flat well out from the weeds.

When the spinner and crankbait bite slows down, switch over to jigs. After the active walleyes are caught those remaining in the weeds will take a bit more enticing to catch. A Jig might not be the best search bait but a well placed jig can trigger a strike from a neutral or dormant walleye. This can make the difference between catching a handful of walleyes and catching a boat load. As usual, the more versatile the angler is the more fish they will catch.

Anglers who just fish the weedline will pass up lots of fish. Over the years I have learned that during the post spawn, weed related walleyes tend to act like largemouth bass. The weeds are sparse and walleye can roam easily through the weeds. I have found post spawn walleyes in as shallow as three feet of water on bright days. During the day, they will use the shade of the weeds to block the sun and they can remain for extended periods of time in shallow water. Later in summer when weedgrowth intensifies, walleyes will hold along the weedlines and avoid dense weed cover.

Why are walleye so shallow in the spring? The answer, quite simply, is food! Contrary to popular belief, walleyes do not always fall into the dreaded post spawn when they remain inactive for weeks. While this does occur on deep, clear infertile lakes, lakes with good weedgrowth will see males walleyes going on the feed within days of completing spawning. If a stable weather pattern moves in after spawn ing, water temperatures will rise and the female walleyes will also start to feed. Remember that the main focal point for forage during the early season is fresh weeds.

Every walleye angler knows that jigs take weed walleyes during the early season, but most anglers use too small of a presentation. Being bass fishermen, I have caught many an early summer walleye with bass jigs in the weeds. With bass jigs having a much larger profile than walleye jigs, it did not take me long to realize that a larger profile jig will catch more and larger weed walleyes. I have refined my bass tactics into walleye tactics when fishing weed related wall-eyes.

Weed walleyes caught with large jigs

By larger profile I am referring to the overall size of the presentation and not a heavier weight. For the most part we are fishing in water less than six feet in depth; too heavy of a jig will drop too fast and get lost in the weeds. What I have done over the years is taken a leadhead jig with an oversized hook and tied on a small rubber skirt. On the shank of the jig I attach a three inch ribbed grub and tip the jig with a leech or grub. The ribbed grub gives the jig a slow fall, which will trigger a strike from any walleye. If walleyes are biting hard, you won't need to tip the jig with any live bait.

The skirt adds both color and vibration. I use brighter skirts and grubs on my jigs for walleye than I would for bass since walleyes tend to be attracted to brighter colors than bass. Chartreuse, yellow, orange and hot pink are good skirt colors and my grubs are chartreuse, white and orange. Sometimes I have caught walleyes on strange color combinations that no self respecting bass would have given a second glance. However, both walleye and bass are attracted to the vibration the rubber skirt gives off when being jigged through the weeds.

When jigging for weed walleyes I usually upgrade the size of my line. This might sound taboo to walleye anglers who are used to finesse presentations. By using eight pound test line, instead of six pound test line, the jig will sink a bit slower. Braided lines will also work well for jigging the weeds since they let the angler feel the slightest pick up. When jigging the weeds, keep in mind that walleyes are scattered throughout the water column and not bottom related. The longer your offering is in the strike zone the more walleyes you will catch.

Small lakes that do produce big walleyes will have a smaller walleye population but a larger size structure. While you won't catch a boat load of hawgs, trophy potential is possible. Most of these are oligotrophic lakes that contain clear water and are infertile. One 250 acre lake, whose name I will not reveal, has been a favorite of mine over the years. This lake has produced walleyes in excess of

10 pounds on many occasions. The water is extremely clear, weeds are restricted to a few shoreline areas and structure is at a premium. A few fish cribs have been submerged in the lake over the years in hopes to create some fish habitat.

There is no stocking in the lake since natural reproduction seems to be sufficient. As far as I can tell, 100 percent of the walleyes spawn on the pronounced shoreline point in the center of the lake. The point tops off at 8 feet and one side of the point tappers down to 30 feet while the other side of the point drops sharply down to 40 feet. The edges and base of the point are granite while the top is broken rock and gravel. If a person created a lake, they could not design a more perfect piece of structure.

After spawning, many walleyes remain on the edges and the base of the point during the day and move atop the point to feed after dark. The top of the point is where spawning occurs and a variety of minnow species, perch, smallmouth and panfish move in to feed on the walleye fry. There is more activity in this one spot after dark than anywhere else on the lake. Casting shallow running crankbaits in black/silver will produce savage strikes from big walleyes. It is an easy pattern to catch a few big walleyes, but since I prefer to avoid fishing after dark, I kept this from my clients.

I have taken many of my clients to this lake over the years, but only on overcast days with light winds. If these conditions prevail, walleyes will remain on the top of the point throughout the day. The only difference being the crankbait bit is limited, so a combination of crankbaits and live bait is needed. I would position my boat parallel to the point with my electric trolling motor and make perpendicular casts over the point. It was repetitious each May when I fished the point. Catch a few big walleyes on a crankbait and switch over to a jig and minnow and catch more walleyes, although they would run smaller. This one two punch, allowed me to keep many a client happy.

I seldom guide on the lake on a sunny day but when I do my clients usually manage to put plenty of walleyes in the boat. Since trolling is not allowed on the lake, jigging is the best presentation. If it is not too windy I use my electric trolling motor to move me along the edge of the point, vertical jigging along the deep rocks. While vertical jigging it is important to keep an eye on your electronics to look for suspended walleyes. When you locate suspended walleyes you need to raise your jig to connect with the feeding walleyes.

Another tactic when walleyes are suspended off a point is to rig up a slip bobber at the desired depth with a leech or minnow. When rigging a slip bobber for suspended walleyes you will need to set the bait at the exact depth. Walleyes suspending off a point are not prone to move up or down in the water column to hit a presentation. You will have only about twelve to fourteen inches to play with so spend a few minutes and do it right.

Walleyes suspended off structure are far more cooperative than walleyes suspending over open water.
If the wind is right, drifting along the edge of the point can be productive. While drifting can be great if you are fishing a flat, when you trying to fish an exact spot it can be tough. The biggest problem with drifting is that you are at the mercy of the wind and you have little control over your direction and speed. When drifting I rely on a slip sinker rig with either a plain hook or floating jighead. If walleyes are tight to the bottom, I use a plain hook but if they are suspended I use a floating jighead. Try to keep the bait as tight to the point as possible, since this is where the bulk of the walleyes will be located.

Once I catch a walleye on a drift, I immediately toss out a floating marker. Don't stop your drift, because you might drift into more walleyes. If you drift a while and catch another walleye, toss out another floating marker. This will enable you to mark several spots instead of concentrating on just one. Continue to make drifts between the markers if possible. If the action slows, go back to the floating markers, drop anchor and jig. If you would have dropped anchor on the first spot where you caught a walleye, you might not have caught walleyes in the other spots.

While I have caught lots of walleye off the point in May and early June, the big walleyes I have caught all came from the fish cribs. As with fishing weed walleyes, I refined most of my fish crib tactics from what I have learned from bass fishing. This particular lake has a good smallmouth bass population but I don't think I have ever seen anyone fishing for them. Most of the people fishing on the lake are chasing walleyes and panfish.

John was one of my regular clients and he had booked me for three days of smallmouth bass fishing. Each year John fished with me I would try to take him to at least one new place. Not that John didn't catch fish in the old spots, he just liked the idea of expanding his horizons. When I picked John up in the morning it was overcast and there was a light breeze. I told him we were going to a clear water walleye lake that has a sleeper smallmouth bass population that few people knew about. I told John that the lake had limited cover and that we would primarily be fishing fish cribs.

Well, so much for the overcast skies and a slight breeze! By the time we got to the boat landing we had bluebird skies and no wind. I told John that the conditions had changed and we were looking at less than ideal conditions. Since John had not fished the lake before we agreed to give it a shot. So I launched the boat and headed out of the shallow bay towards a series of fish cribs on the north shoreline of the lake. On the ride to the fish cribs, I thought to myself that although we did not have ideal conditions, we did have the lake to ourselves.

I stopped the boat well out from the fish cribs and put down the electric trolling motor. John tied on a medium depth crankbait on one rod and on another I gave him a darter head jig and a three inch watermelon grub. John made a few casts with his crankbait and caught a 15 inch smallmouth. He continued to catch a bunch of smallmouth all in the 15 inch class. I told him to grab his rod with the grub and I would move closer to the fish crib. John caught a few more smallmouth and eventually I worked the boat in until we were right over the crib.

Walleye caught on the edge of a fish crib

As the shadow of the boat drifted over the crib, I looked down to see two behemoth walleyes holding tight to the outside edge of the crib. I yelled to John to look off the starboard side of the boat to the bottom of the crib. Next, I grabbed one of my rods which was rigged with a number four live bait hook and put on a lively leech. We were in 15 feet of water and we could see the big walleyes as plain as day. I gave the rod to john and told him to let the leech drop down to the walleyes. Both of us watched the leech hit one of the big walleyes right between the eyes. The leech slid off the nose of the walleye and it did not make a move. John repeated this procedure but the results were the same. I guess the big walleye was not hungry.

We kept fishing the cribs and continued to catch 15 inch smallmouth the rest of the day. We also continued to see large walleyes relating to about one third of the fish cribs. The walleyes were all holding on the deep water edge of the fish cribs where they were shaded by the crib itself. I told John that they were not relating to the fish crib for food, but due to the shade it was a comfort zone on sunny days. John kept trying to catch one of those walleyes but his efforts were to no avail. One walleye sucked in the leech and spit it out before John could react to set the hook.

Even though walleyes relate to these fish cribs on sunny days, they are tough to catch and finesse presentations are very much in order. A light one sixteenth ounce leadhead jig tipped with a minnow or leech is my highest percentage presentation. When casting light jigs I use a seven foot medium light action rod with a fast tip. The longer rod will allow you to attain maximum casting distance and the fast tip will allow you to react to the slightest pick up. You need to position the boat as far away as possible and still be able to cast to the edge of the fish crib. If you are close enough to see the fish, you are too close and will not catch a big walleye. I use a seven foot rod and four pound fluorocarbon line. The fluorocarbon line is invisible under water and it has no stretch. The lack of stretch in the line will allow for a good hookset and the sensitivity of the fluorocarbon line will let you feel the slightest pickup. It is amazing how a big walleye can suck in a one sixteenth ounce jig without the angler sensing anything. After all, look at how John saw a big walleye suck in the bait yet couldn't set the hook before the walleye refused the bait.

Over the years I had fished those cribs many times with a jig and minnow or a jig and leech and caught many a big walleye. If I would not have accidentally stumbled upon those big walleyes on that bright sunny day while fishing for smallmouth, I would never have found this pattern.

Natural lakes have long been steady walleye producers in the spring. Living in the Northwood's I am fortunate to have plenty of excellent walleye lakes within a short drive from my home. The key is to know when to hit a particular lake and when to leave a lake alone. Spend as much time on the water, since this kind of knowledge is only gained from experience and paying your dues on the water.

Chapter Five
Summer River walleyes

Most rivers with decent walleye populations see consistent action through the summer months. Those same river walleyes that traveled long distances to spawn in the spring are dispersed throughout the river system. Locating walleyes in summer can pose a problem at times but once you find them, unlike their lake cousins, they usually bite. This is not to say that summer river walleyes aren't finicky at times, but for the most part it's all about Location!

All rivers don't produce walleyes in the summer since the river might only have a marginal walleye population. Stick with rivers that are known to produce walleyes in the spring since these rivers will hold the highest population of fish. If you feel adventurous, or just want to avoid other fisherman, then try the lesser-known smaller rivers. These rivers will often yield good catches since they receive less fishing pressure. However, in mid-summer water levels can be low and navigation can be a problem on smaller rivers. You might have trouble catching legal sized walleyes from smaller rivers.

Summer river walleyes

Even though the bulk of the walleyes have left the spawning areas in summer, a certain percentage of walleyes are not too far from spawning areas. The tail waters below a dam will always hold a walleye population regardless of the season and should be one of the first places to fish. There is plenty of current regardless of the water level, and forage is plentiful. The water released through the dam is colder than on other sections of the river as well as being more oxygenated. All of these factors combine for excellent walleye habitat with the only thing missing in summer being walleye fishermen. For some unknown reason, some dams receive heavy pressure in the spring but are deserted in the summer.

Dams will offer walleyes a constant food supply of small baitfish, panfish and crayfish. The water level of the river will be the main factor in determining walleye location. If water levels are low, which they usually are in summer, walleyes can stack up in the deep holes below a dam. Walleyes will hold in these holes during the day and move shallow after dark to feed on crayfish and minnows. If a sufficient food supply is present, walleyes will have no need to vacate the area.

Many dams generate power and there will be periods of high and low water. Expect major feeding periods to occur when water levels begin to rise. As the water level rises, the baitfish and crayfish will be flushed out of their haunts and begin to move shallow. Walleyes and smallmouth will not be far behind as they sense an easy meal as they also head for shallow water. Since power is usually generated on a schedule, you will be able to plan your fishing to these periods. Prime periods for generating power are from noon to late afternoon.

During periods of rising water take advantage of the high walleye activity. Walleyes can be so aggressive that they can strike a crankbait as hard as a smallmouth. A crankbait will enable you to cover water quickly and lets you pick off the active fish one by one. This is one time when you can forget about the walleyes that won't hit the aggressive presentation. You are better off keeping on the move instead of sitting in one spot.

Although walleyes are feeding on crayfish, crayfish imitation crankbaits are not the best choice for walleyes. They are great for smallmouth bass but walleyes prefer to hit brighter colored crankbaits. This is yet another walleye pattern that I discovered while smallmouth fishing. This color pattern has only let me down a few times.

One time in mid-July, my clients and I were catching smallmouth with topwater baits and plastics when the water level on the river began to rise. As the current began to increase, the topwater bite came to an abrupt halt and the pickups on our plastics became fewer and lighter. Before we knew it we were catching nothing. I had my trolling motor on the highest speed in an attempt to deal with the increased current and I had all I could do to hold my boat in the swiftly moving water. I knew that we had to change our game plan and fast.

We were on fish so I was trying to avoid a major move. In one last effort, I told my clients to tie on a crayfish imitation crankbait. They had plenty of crankbaits of their own so I did not see the baits they chose to tie on since my all my efforts were being expended in controlling the boat. As we slipped downriver, my clients began pounding the shoreline and it did not take long for one of them to catch a 17 inch smallmouth on the crayfish imitation crankbait. He released the smallmouth and in a matter of a few casts caught another smallmouth.

Within a few minutes the second client had a fish on but to our surprise it was an 18 inch walleye. As I netted the walleye I observed the fire tiger crankbait hanging from the walleye's mouth. I put the walleye in the live well and I thought that if my clients did not want it, I would have the walleye for supper. The action continued and both my clients kept catching fish. The guy with the crawfish imitation crankbait caught smallmouth and the guy with the fire tiger crankbait caught walleyes. The crankbaits they were using had similar action, they were short and had a wide wobble, but the color was definitely different. While it is a logical pattern, I had never seen a situation where one species would only hit a specific color crankbait.

Since that day some twenty odd years ago, I have been using these crankbait color patterns for the targeted species during the summer. It only seems to hold true for periods of rising water, either through surges below the dam or heavy rains. During stable river conditions there does not seem to be a color preference in crankbaits between walleyes and smallmouth. Obviously, this might just be a pattern for the Menominee River, since I have not tried it on any other rivers. However when you are smallmouth fishing and want a few walleyes for the pan, give it a try.

If you can't locate walleyes below the dam, just like in spring, try the first deep hole below the dam. Summer walleyes will stack up in the holes but they will be a bit tougher to catch than in the spring. The biggest problem is that walleyes don't tend to advertise themselves in deep water. Even though the river might have a rock bottom, silt will wash into the hole and when walleye relate to a muck bottom, they are harder to pick up on a locator. The hole may be full of debris which will also make locating walleyes more difficult.

River walleyes do spend a great deal of time in deep water during summer. On one river deep water can be 20 feet while on another river 10 feet could be the deepest available water source. On most rivers there is sufficient forage in deep water and walleyes can stack up big time. When they stack up in deep water, they will be easy to see with your electronics. You can expect to see different sized fish holding at a different depth. The more variances in the depth the more active the walleyes will be. If they are all holding tightly to the bottom, they could be tough to catch.

Another advantage to deep water river walleyes is that the bite can be consistent even at high noon. More importantly than the actual time, look for the activity level to increase after any change in the conditions. If it is overcast and the sun comes out, walleyes will make a move. By the same token if you have clear skies and cloud cover moves in, walleye will make a move. Anything that stirs the pot will cause walleyes to move which means light strikes change into hard strikes.

Deep water walleyes are easier to entice than walleyes relating to deep water in lakes and large reservoirs. Once you locate walleyes with your electronics the same vertical jigging techniques will work. The big difference is that your jigs should be tipped with leeches and crawlers instead of minnows. When vertical jigging, I also like to drag a line on the bottom with a healthy nightcrawler. Many times I have had short strikes while vertical jigging only to have a walleye savagely attack a nightcrawler. When you feel a strike on the crawler give it a few seconds before you set the hook.

In spring, I continue to vertical jig after I catch a few walleyes. However, in summer, if I pick up a walleye while vertical jigging I will drop an anchor to hold me in the spot. This allows me to pursue other presentations and catch more walleyes. Summer walleyes don't seem to be as zeroed in on just one presentation. Besides, when fishing a nightcrawler on the bottom I like to keep the boat in a stationary position. I use just enough weight on the nightcrawler rig to keep it on the bottom. This method has resulted in many large walleyes.

While you can catch walleyes relating to deep water, I prefer to concentrate on walleyes that move to shallow water to feed. By concentrating on the restaurant you will be dealing with walleyes that are out to lunch instead of taking a nap. Feeding walleyes are more likely to make mistakes and they will also hit bait with more intensity. Even though river walleyes are by nature more aggressive than lake walleyes, the shallower you can fish for them the more of them you will catch.

You will find the most active walleyes relating to midriver structure. Exact walleye location will depend on the smallmouth bass population. If smallmouth bass are the dominant specie in the river, walleye will be pushed into secondary areas. A rocky weedy mid-river shelf could be crawling with crayfish and minnows but also loads of small-mouth. Walleyes in turn will relate to the downstream side of the shelf as it drops down to deeper water. Walleyes are relating to the same structure as the smallmouth, only slightly deeper. If the river has only a small smallmouth population look for the walleye to be out full force in the rocks.

When fishing rocks for river walleye, you need to learn to fish the shadows. Just as when fishing rock ledges in reservoirs mid-river walleyes relate to the shadows of mid-river rocks. The big difference is that reservoir walleyes are permanent fixtures within the rocks but river walleye are more aggressive and will chase a crankbait. Cast bright colored crankbaits around the rocks just like you would if you were fishing for smallmouth. Ideally, the crankbait should run deeply enough to bump off the rocks, since bumping off the rocks will trigger a strike.

Walleyes caught in the shadows

Jigs are the most consistent presentations when fishing summer river walleyes. If walleyes are active there is no need for live bait and a jig and twister tail will do the trick. When the dam is closed and water flow is at a minimum go with a 1/8th-ounce jig. On bright days I rely on silver or copper plated jigs. On overcast days gold produces the best. I fish the jigs on a medium light action rod with eight pound test fluorocarbon/nylon hybrid line. This line has limited stretch and allows for light jigs to reach the bottom in the current. Plain fluorocarbon line has memory and it does not work well with light baits when using a spinning reel.

One plus factor is many dams can be fished from a boat or from the shore. In fact, it is common to see bank fishermen out produce those fishing from a boat. Rock and rubble can make navigation tough under low water conditions. By fishing or wading from shore, you can get right on top of the walleyes. However, if you are wading, use extreme caution. Fishing the deep hole below the dam can also be productive, especially in the middle of the day. Here too, wading is an effective method.

One summer walleye hot spot is rocks or an island on the inside bend in a river. The island or exposed rock does not need to be large, just big enough to break the current. If it is in shallow water the odds are it will be a hot spot for smallmouth bass, but if it has water deeper than 8 feet adjacent to the structure walleyes will likely be present. Walleyes will hold tight to the bottom and smallmouth will suspend, so it is easy to distinguish the different location of the two species.

One of the best walleye fishing days I have ever had in summer was when a few clients and I were fishing a small island on the Menominee River in late July. I had been catching a ton of smallmouth tight to the rocks but that day my clients wanted walleyes. I positioned my boat about 60 feet out from the rock and my locator showed fish everywhere. Most of the fish we marked were within two feet of the bottom but a few were suspended. I showed the locator to my clients and they were all fired up.

I eased down the anchor in 10 feet of water and told my clients that we would be fishing on both sides of the boat. I instructed one of the guys to tie on a 1/8 ounce orange jig and tip it with a leech and the other guy to tie on a number four live bait hook rigged with a nightcrawler. The guy with the jig and leech cast towards the island and the guy with the crawler cast on the deep water side of the boat.

It did not take long for the nightcrawler to produce a 14 inch walleye. The jig and leech produced nothing and after the guy with the nightcrawler caught his fifth walleye his friend decided to change. The action was so hot with the nightcrawlers I suggested that my clients use half a crawler in hopes of conserving bait. The walleyes continued to hammer the half nightcrawler and everything looked great.

The action continued throughout the morning but I suddenly realized that we were running short of nightcrawlers. One of the guys put on a leech but could not even get a nibble. I tried some plastics and I also could not coax a strike. It was a nightcrawler bite and that was it. The only problem was that it was only 11:00 am and we were out of bait. I told my clients that I knew of a place that wasn't far that sold nightcrawlers. It did not take long for us to decide that if our success was to continue, we needed more nightcrawlers.

We headed back to the boat landing and one of my clients stayed with the boat and one came with me to check out the nightcrawler sign I had passed many times on the county highway. We drove to the sign and pulled into a gravel driveway and came upon an old trailer, surrounded by a bunch of old farm buildings that had not been touched for years. Farm and logging equipment, trucks, tractors and piles of junk were scattered everywhere. The place looked a bit spooky and as I walked up to the trailer I did not know who or what to expect. In the back of my mind I was expecting some burly old dude with bib overalls who hadn't had a change of clothes in years. To my surprise an old lady well into her 80's opened the door and pleasantly asked, "Can I help you?" I said, "We saw the sign on the road and wondered if you had any nightcrawlers." She went into the back and brought back two containers and she said, "This is all I have."

She said I owed her four dollars, so I gave her a five dollar bill and told her to keep the change. We had to settle for four dozen nightcrawlers since we cleaned out the bait shop. The old woman had just made her big sale for the week and probably headed back behind the old barn to dig up a few more dozen nightcrawlers. I am sure this was not a production job, and all she needed was a few dozen on hand to make some spending money.

With two containers of nightcrawlers we headed back to the small island and anchored in the exact spot. All three of us made several casts but could not even feel a light pick up. We all looked at each other and shrugged our shoulders and I said that the walleyes were gone. I suggested to my clients that we make a move since it was likely that the reason the walleyes had moved was either that a few big pike or a musky had moved into the area, or else that all the baitfish were gone. One of my clients did not want to budge since this was the most fantastic walleye fishing he had ever had. We tried several other spots but the only thing we caught was a few small walleyes on leeches. That day we boated over 70 walleyes from that small rock island on the Menominee River. We never did need those extra nightcrawlers.

Submerged rocks on the inside bend of a river might only cover a small area, but since they are difficult for anglers to locate, they usually result in great fishing. These are the little ace in the hole spots that a guide only divulges when the fishing is tough and your reputation is on the line. The client has to think that these places are really tough to locate or better yet, you let them think it is another spot that you just happened to stumble on. Of course, when you leave the spot you manage to let them think that the spot will be void of fish the next day.

**Mark Zoellick with walleyes
caught on nightcrawlers**

One August day, I had to visit one of my favorite walleye spots. We had caught about 50 nice smallmouth that day but my client inquired as to the possibility of taking home a few walleyes for supper. That was fine except we were fishing in a section of the river that has but a marginal walleye population. I knew of one good spot but I was fishing with a client who had a cabin in the area and under those circumstances I would rather not reveal my hotspot. We already had a great day of smallmouth fishing and I could have taken my client to a spot where we might have caught a few walleyes. If we did not catch any walleyes I could just chalk it up to the finicky walleye bite. Needless to say, in trying to the best job I can for my clients, we slid into one of my all time favorite walleye spots in order to salvage the day.

The spot is perfect, the river makes a sharp turn and on the inside bend of the river is a rock ledge that just scratches the surface during low water conditions. As the river rises you can see the riffles but most anglers think it is a boulder and avoid the spot. What they do not know is that the inside edge is a series of erratic rock ledges that have many crevasses that sharply plunge to 10 feet. Besides being a current break, these crevasses also block the sunlight and can hold a ton of walleyes in an area that is no bigger than a garage.

It is a simple pattern once you study the water level and the current. If the current is swift, walleyes will be holding along the ledge, and during low water or moderate current walleyes will hold in the hole. On that particular day that I arrived on the spot, the current was perfect for fishing the crevasses. If there was less current the fish would be in the deep hole and if there was more current the walleyes would be holding on the downstream edge of the rocks, just out of the main current.

Due to the current it would be impossible to hold with my trolling motor. I moved about 30 feet upstream from the rock ledge and carefully dropped the anchor. The anchor immediately held in the current and I let the boat drift until we were over the ledge and tied off the anchor rope. Even though I knew walleyes were present, my electronics did not pick them up since the walleyes were holding in the crevasses.

I told my client to toss a 1/8th ounce orange leadhead jig tipped with a crawler at the riffle. He followed my advice and to his disgust he did not catch a walleye but instead buried the jig in the rocks. He quickly snapped his line and I suggested that he try a 1/16 ounce orange jig and tip it with half of a nightcrawler. He again followed my advice and in under a minutes' time he was fighting a 16 inch walleye. We netted the walleye, placed it in the livewell and continued to catch 3 more legal walleyes and several undersized ones. Considering the big smallmouth we had boated earlier in the day, it was an entirely successful outing.

While we caught lots of walleyes that afternoon, I did not let my client know that we were fishing the side of the rock ledge as opposed to the hole. I knew if he returned to the spot the conditions would be different and walleyes would be holding in a slightly different location. I guess if he wants to know where the walleyes went, he will have to read this book.

My Father with summer river walleyes

After heavy summer rains, walleye fishing on rivers can be tough for some anglers. However, this is one of my favorite scenarios in which to fish for walleyes. As the water level rises and the current intensifies, walleyes move shallow. During high water look for shoreline weeds to be where the action is. Unlike smallmouth and largemouth bass which can be pushed into the weeds during high water periods, walleyes will hold very tight to the edge of the weeds, regardless of the depth. I have seen walleyes as shallow as three feet on a bright sunny day, under high water.

Why are walleyes so shallow under these conditions? The answer is food. As the volume of water increases, the baitfish are pushed away from deeper cover and scramble to avoid the current. Some baitfish will find comfort in deep cover but most of them will be pushed to the surface and eventually gravitate toward shoreline areas. An angler with a good eye can locate large schools of baitfish surfacing tight to shoreline weeds. The surfacing baitfish will be just out of the main current flow with bass, walleye and pike all taking advantage of an easy meal.

Smallmouth and largemouth bass will move extremely shallow and can be within inches of the shoreline. Smaller pike will be in the weeds while the larger pike and walleyes will move into the edge of the weeds with the least amount of current. What anglers don't realize is that, as they cast the shallows for bass, they can be passing up a load of walleyes. With the baitfish also trying to find comfort in the rising water, walleyes will make a connection and go on a feeding rampage. These are actively feeding walleyes that will even hit a spinnerbait aimed at a big bass.

If you are looking for walleyes, drift along the shoreline casting minnow imitation crankbaits along the weed edge. Make your cast parallel to the shoreline and keep the crank bait tight to the weeds. When making your retrieve, hold your rod tip up high. By keeping your rod tip up high, the crankbait will ride just high enough to keep you out of the heavy weeds. If you pick up weeds on every cast, switch to a shallower running crankbait. Use a steady retrieve and give the crankbait an occasional twitch. Remember these are active walleyes and a short twitch can trigger a strike.

30" summer river walleye

Look for the downstream side of an island to hold the mother load of walleyes. Weeds are usually abundant on the back side of an island due to the slack water during normal or low water levels. Walleyes will usually feed in these weeds early and late in the day as well as after dark. With the rising water more baitfish move into the area, and I have sometimes witnessed walleyes feeding on the surface like bass. It is an amazing sight to see and just awesome if you are a walleye fisherman. I have even caught a few walleyes on surface baits while fishing for smallmouth behind an island.

The back side of an island can see both smallmouth bass and walleyes feeding at the same time. Just as along the shoreline, bass will be roaming the weeds and walleyes will be holding along the weedline. When searching for walleyes try a crankbait and when you locate walleyes switch to live bait presentations. However, there have been times when walleye activity level is high and there is no need for live bait.

By fishing a river you will not only catch fish but also find peace and quiet. Most lakes see plenty of recreational boating in summer, and besides creating noise, the increased commotion can make a tough walleye bite even tougher. On a river you will be able to relax and catch walleye at the same time.

Chapter Six
Summer Walleyes In Lakes & Reservoirs

While most of my summer is spent in pursuit of smallmouth and musky, on occasion I have guided for walleye. These guide trips were usually with people wanting to learn a particular body of water where they were staying for their vacation. For the most part they were literally here to enjoy summer and they realized that it is not a prime time for walleye fishing. My clients don't expect to catch a wallhanger, but they would like to have a few meals of tasty walleye fillets on their vacation. The problem that can arise is that they are staying on a specific lake and since they are using my services to learn that lake, I can't take them a few miles down the road to a better lake. You are really at a disadvantage if the lake they are staying on is a poor fishing lake. So you head out on the water at sunup and hope to catch the early morning bite and usually spend most of the day catching bass, pike or anything that bites.

Big summer walleye

There has been more than one guide trip on a lake where my clients would question the ability of their guide due to the lack of fish put in the boat. However, they darn near demanded that I take them out on the lake where they were staying and not another lake, even if I had told them the other lake was loaded with fish. I guess they just figure that I simply wave my magic wand and make the fish jump into the boat. They just assume that every lake has a hot spot that is loaded with fish. Of course, these are usually people with limited experience who, not coincidentally, often don't have the patience to learn.

Summer walleye fishing doesn't need to be something that you enter into with low expectations. While summer walleye are by no means easy to pattern, they are catchable and you can land a wallhanger. Just like in the spring, you need to fish the proper water along with trying to fish the water during the peak feeding periods. Summer walleye are even more finicky and exhibit distinct feeding patterns from which they seldom veer. The most predictable feeding pattern characteristic to walleyes is to feed after dark. While night feeding walleyes are the norm on most waters in summer, they really hold their own on clear water lakes, especially those known for producing trophy walleyes. As I stated in the previous chapter, night fishing is not in my blood although I have done my share of it over the years due to necessity. In July and August, when daytime temperatures can climb into the nineties, fishing after dark might be the only way to catch walleyes. Sometimes you do what you have to whether you like it or not.

Deep clear water lakes will see very little walleye activity during the day. Walleyes are either holding tight to the bottom, suspended over deep water, holding tight to fish cribs or shoreline wood, or buried tight to the weeds. Wherever they are holding, one thing is certain, they are probably not feeding. Add in a bit of annoying boat traffic and a walleye angler's odds of catching even a few walleyes are slim to none. Along with not catching any fish, your sanity will also be tested and you won't enjoy your day on the water. This is one of those times when I can honestly tell an angler to go find another place to fish. They are in the wrong place at the wrong time.

An angler could fish that same lake after dark and enter into a different world. Gone are the jet skis and water skiers, and better yet, the walleye will be on the feed. This isn't to say that there will be nights when walleye do not cooperate, but, in general, if the angler has a good handle on the lake, they should connect with walleyes. By changing their timing they are now on the right lake at the right time.

While walleye location is usually not a problem, peak feeding periods are, and these feeding periods can vary from lake to lake. Some lakes will see a surge in walleye activity right at dusk and the action will continue for a few hours and then abruptly stop. On another lake it might take a few hours of darkness before walleyes are stimulated to feed. Generally the clearer the water the longer it will take for walleyes to become active. Another deciding factor is the amount of boat traffic on the lake. If boat traffic is limited during the day there could be a major feeding period at dusk. If the lake has intense boat traffic during the day it could take hours before walleyes are motivated to feed.

Weeds are the key to night feeding walleyes. Baitfish will stack up in the first few yards from the weedline and if the weeds are not too dense, they will move into the weeds themselves. Approach the weedline with caution, being careful not to spook the walleyes. A prior knowledge of the weedline is essential. Often the largest walleyes will be suspending off the edge of the weeds and even though they are actively feeding, they are easily spooked. Just like when I am working a shoreline for bass, when fishing weeds for walleye, I start on the deeper edge and move shallow. A bit of caution always results in bigger fish regardless of the specie.

Start working a crankbait along the weedline with a slow steady retrieve. Try different retrieves until the right one is found. If the crankbait does not produce or you're getting short strikes, try a suspending jerkbait. Use a series of short vigorous strikes to get a walleye's attention and then use short slow twitches to trigger the strike. Many walleye anglers use suspended jerkbaits when trolling, but here in the Northwood's, trolling is illegal and few anglers realize their casting potential. This is just another bass presentation that will catch walleyes.

You can forget about finesse presentations for night biting walleyes since they are on the prowl. My first choice in baits for night fishing is a shallow running crankbait with a wide lip and a rattle. The more noise the crankbait emits the harder the walleye strike will be. As far as color goes, stick with dark crankbaits such as black/silver or blue/silver. The less of a silhouette the crankbait has the better.

Even spinnerbaits will catch night feeding walleyes. I learned this pattern while smallmouth fishing many years ago. I was fishing a weed bed a few hours after dark when my client tossed out a 3/8 ounce black spinnerbait and connected with a 9-pound walleye. He had been buzzing the spinnerbait over the weeds and the big walleye hit the spinnerbait within seconds of it hitting the water. It was one of those nights when baitfish were surfacing everywhere around us. My client continued to cast the spinnerbaits wherever he heard surfacing baitfish and continued to catch big walleyes. My client did not catch his trophy small-mouth that night but he did take home the 9 pound walleye to put on his wall. I have never seen a hot spinnerbait bite since that night, but I have had clients catch an occasional big walleye on spinnerbaits, and on rare occasion I have caught walleyes on buzzbaits. One thing is certain, when a walleye hits a spinnerbait or a buzz bait, they are big!

If the lake you choose to fish has a mid-lake hump, this may be the big walleye spot. I have fished hundreds of clear water lakes and have seen only a few that did not have at least one off shore hump. These humps will usually have a rock base with a combination of large boulders, gravel and sand. Some humps will sprout heavy weedgrowth while others are completely absent of weeds. If a lake has signifi-cant weedgrowth in shoreline areas, this will cause wall-eyes to spread out when they go on the feed. Walleyes that are relating to a hump will be concentrated in a smaller area and thus easier to locate.

However, if weeds are at a premium in the lake the hump can be where all the action is. Even if the mid-lake hump is void of weedgrowth it can be a buffet after dark. Perch and a variety of types of baitfish will move atop the hump and walleye will not be far behind. The only problem that you will encounter is that, besides walleyes, the hump can attract smallmouth bass, northern pike and muskies. If muskies are present, don't expect to find too many active walleyes.

Big walleye caught on an isolated hump

Larger humps will attract more walleyes, but not necessarily the largest ones. A small isolated hump can attract a few monster walleyes especially if it has quick access to deep water. I began fishing these isolated humps to avoid other anglers. Large humps are easy to locate and it doesn't take anglers long to realize the spots' potential. Smaller humps are more difficult to find but worth the extra effort. The problem with fishing a smaller hump is that most anglers spook the larger walleyes since they head right for the top of the hump. Just like with the weed walleyes, the larger walleyes can suspend off the side of the hump feeding on baitfish. In fact, although the hump is what attracts the forage, the larger walleyes might not ever see the top of the hump.

A GPS will be a great aid in locating the hump. Even an angler who is very familiar with a lake might have trouble locating a hump after dark. The GPS will also allow the angler to spot the boat well away from the hump allowing you to catch the big stragglers on the edge of the hump. If the wind is light, start casting crankbaits along the edges of the hump and when you get atop the hump switch over to a shallow running crankbait. If there is no wind, use your electric trolling motor to move you atop the hump.

If trolling is allowed then you will be able to cover water effectively and catch more walleyes. Start trolling around well out from the hump with crankbaits that dive to different depths. Try to cover the water column effectively. Gradually decrease the area you are trolling until you are right on the edge of the hump. If the hump is shallower than five feet, avoid trolling over the hump and opt to kill the motor and cast. This will increase your chances of catching larger walleyes.

Summer walleyes can be caught on natural lakes in summer during the day, but again much will depend on the individual lakes. I have fished several lakes where active walleyes can roam the deep weeds. Shallow weeds might hold largemouth bass and panfish during the day but not walleyes. However, once you get below the 10 foot depth, you start to lose some light penetration even on clear lakes. The shadow of the weeds creates a comfort zone for both walleyes and bait fish. A good locator is a must to locate both the weedlines and the fish. Search for clouds of bait-fish as a key to walleye location.

A variety of weed types can hold walleye but cabbage is the most desirable. Milfoil for example can attract wall-eyes if it is the dominant weed in the lake, but it is very tough to fish. By mid-summer, it is impossible to get a lure or live bait presentation close to the edge of the milfoil without picking up slime or weeds. Cabbage on the other hand is easy to fish since you can work a variety of baits along the edges without getting hung up. Besides being easier to fish, cabbage weed will hold larger schools of baitfish and walleyes. Both live and artificial baits are pro-ductive and both will have their place. If walleyes are active artificial baits will work, but if walleyes are in a neutral mood, you will need to rely on live bait.

Look for outstanding features within the weeds. Wall-eyes like to relate to structure and a weed point is just as much structure as a rock point. The big difference is that most anglers are able to find a shoreline point, but locating a weed point will take a trained eye. The best points will taper to deep water and the weeds will become less dense as the depth increases. Yes, these are haunts for trophy musky but they can also hold a few 30 plus inch walleyes.

When looking for weed walleyes start out with a crank-bait. Start out with a mid-depth crankbait and rip it along the edges of the weeds. Ripping a crankbait will often result in a larger walleye. Through the years I have perfected this method and it has resulted in numerous big walleyes. The crankbait should just dig into the weeds and not drive down to deep. Along with using the right crankbait the proper rod and line is essential. A fiberglass 6' 6" crankbait rod is perfect for ripping through the weeds. After testing a variety of lines I have found that either 10 pound or 12 pound test hybrid monofilament/fluorocarbon line is best for this purpose. The hybrid line will allow the crankbait to get to its maximum depth and stay in the strike zone longer.

If you are targeting large walleyes, choose to fish peak feeding periods since hawg walleyes will move into the weeds at dusk. If I locate and catch walleyes along a deep weedline during the day, there is a fair chance that larger walleyes will move into the area at dusk since the bait fish aren't leaving, unless the baitfish end up in the bellies of hungry walleyes. When you return to the weedline at dusk, crankbaits will still be effective but since you are looking for larger walleyes, upgrade your crankbait one size. Along with the larger crankbait use a faster retrieve. The faster retrieve will also help in triggering a strike from a larger walleye.

Plastics are also effective for weed walleyes. Four inch grub tails and shad bodies rigged weedless on a jighead is the staple of weed walleye anglers. Several manufacturers make jigheads specially designed for rigging plastics weedless for walleyes. Experiment with different colors until you find the preferred combination for that day. Work the jig along the weedline and let it drop to the base of the weeds. This will enable you to catch both the neutral and active walleyes. You will often find smaller walleyes up higher in the water column and larger walleyes at the base of the weeds.

Smart walleye anglers will use both slip bobbers and jigging presentations when using live bait. Working the weeds with slip bobbers and leeches (or nightcrawlers) is very deadly, and on most days this combination will out fish any other presentation. Make sure your bait rides down to the base of the weeds even if they grow in excess of 20 feet. Be sure to toss your slip bobber into any open weed pockets. While these open weed pockets are more likely to hold largemouth or smallmouth bass, if they are close to the weedline they can attract a few walleyes.

Stained water lakes and flowages will see peak walleye feeding periods occurring during low light conditions, but not necessarily after dark. There are several flowages that have a good night bite, but there are many where the night bite is non-existent. Regardless of whether there is a night bite or not, on the flowage one thing is for certain: there is an early morning and an evening bite. These early morning and evening feeding binges are predictable and easy to tap into. The evening bite might be intense but it usually fits into a small time window. The morning bite can be sporadic but it will last for an extended period of time. So if I had to choose one, it would be the morning bite.

Fishing mid-lake humps at the crack of dawn has resulted in many successful walleye guide trips even in the heat of summer. Just as when fishing a hump on a clear lake, the walleyes on a flowage hump are concentrated in a small area. The big difference is that walleyes suspend less off the edges of the hump and relate to the actual hump, while smallmouth bass and muskies are more likely to suspend off the hump. If muskies or smallmouth bass are atop the hump, look for walleyes to be holding along the edges. After smallmouth or muskies leave the hump, walleyes will make a move.

On some flowages walleyes will hit crankbaits, but for the most part live bait presentations get the nod. You might catch a few walleyes with a crankbait, but those same walleyes you catch with the crankbait will also hit live bait. There is also the possibility that if a walleye refuses the crankbait, it might be turned off. So I don't even bother with artificial presentations. It is hard to beat a jumbo leech floated six inches to one foot off the bottom under a slip bobber. Whether the hump tops off at five feet below the surface or ten feet below the surface, I seldom raise my leech more than one foot off the bottom. Walleyes are holding tight to the hump as they search out baitfish and they are not conditioned to move vertically in the water column.

A slip bobber and leech was the ticket

If there is a light breeze or no wind at all, I use my electric trolling motor to position my boat on the edge of the hump. If there is a good chop on the water, anchor the boat upwind so the transom of the boat drifts over the edge of the hump. Although we are fishing the top of the hump, if you get right on the hump you might spook the walleyes. I am so paranoid about spooking walleyes that if the hump is shallower than 5 feet I will not motor over the hump on a calm morning. If I am fishing a hump deeper than 7 feet I might go over the hump and use my locator to see if any walleyes are present. Here again use caution and common sense.

Slip bobbers are not the only presentation for taking early morning walleyes. A light 1/16 or 1/8 ounce leadhead jig tipped with a leech is always good for a few walleyes. Most humps are covered with rocks and debris and the lighter a jig is the more snag resistant it will be. As far as jig color goes, since we are dealing with low light conditions, stick with plain leadhead jigs. They are cheaper and the color on the jighead makes no difference, or as I tell my clients, "lead head jigs are lighter since they are absent of paint." Don't laugh. I have had more than one client believe this story, especially when they start catching walleyes on the plain leadhead jig. When the fishing is good you can get a client to believe just about anything.

Weeds are also hot in summer for early morning flowage walleyes. Walleyes can be particular as to where in the weeds they'll feed. I have had my best results fishing steep drop offs on the edge of shallow bays. The more expansive the bay the more forage that is present, and, the more numerous and bigger the walleyes will be. These weedy drop offs have resulted in many huge walleyes on a few of my favorite flowages.

Many years ago on High Falls Flowage we boated four walleyes over 27 inches and several more over 20 inches in one two hour period. All the big walleyes were released and my client only kept a few 20 inchers for dinner. After the two hour feeding binge we could not even get a strike from a walleye the rest of the day. The walleye bite slowed down so much that we switched tactics and chased a few smallmouth bass. This is a common feast or famine walleye bite, which is typical in mid-summer.

While low light conditions are prime for summer flowage walleyes, they can be caught consistently on most days. Stained water walleyes are not as finicky during daylight hours as their clear water cousins. Light penetration is not as intense on stained water lakes like it is in clear water. Light penetration in stained water also creates shadows on certain types of structure. Once you learn how walleyes relate to these shadows you can learn how and where to catch them.

Walleyes at mid-day

The first place I search for summer flowage walleyes during the day is neck-down areas and rock ledges. A neck-down area is any area of the flowage where it narrows. This is usually a rocky area with steep shoreline and boulders. The rock ledges and boulders create shadows and walleyes can move into these shadows and stack up like cord wood.

A neck-down area can also have current which will enhance the potential of the spot.

When fishing the shadows within the rocks, you will need to cast a jig and leech right into the shadow. These rock related walleyes will hold tightly into the shade and they don't want to move into the sunlight even for a fast meal. Since you are not using your electronics to locate walleyes, you are not sure if any are present. It will take patience to fish the shadows within the rocks, but don't spend too much time in one area even if you catch a walleye. Walleyes will be scattered and you will seldom find more than two or three walleyes in one area.

One mid-day hotspot that is overlooked by many anglers is the area above the dam. Walleyes will scatter in the deep water above a dam but for the most part are in a neutral or negative mood. You will mark them with your locator but they are tough to catch. However, once the dam starts to generate power, walleyes become more aggressive. Baitfish will begin to panic and small perch holding on the bottom will also start to move. The more water passing through the turbines, the more active the walleyes will be. This has been one of my little secrets for years as people could not figure out when I would decide to fish above the power house.

Summer walleye fishing is much more unpredictable than in the spring. However, while the fishing might not be easy at times, it is every bit a challenge. If you have an open mind and pay attention to a few details, even with a few tough days you should eventually be able to catch a bunch of walleyes.

Chapter Seven
Fall Walleyes

    If you are in pursuit of a wallhanger walleye, then spend as much time as possible fishing in the fall. Each year there are many trophy walleyes caught in the Northwood's by unsuspecting anglers fishing for other species. Musky hunters in particular occasionally find a big walleye hanging on the end of their jerkbait or crankbait. The angler that is prepared and knows the water that they are fishing can expect big things in the fall.

I like to break up the fall into the early and late fall periods. Things progress quickly in the fall and each type of water is affected differently. Rivers for example see quality walleye fishing through the entire fall period and the action in the early fall is passed up by many anglers. Deep clear natural lakes on the other hand can be affected by a turnover that can create havoc and make fishing tough during the early fall. However, prior to ice up, walleyes can go on a feeding binge and the action can be fast and furious.

The start of the fall period is dictated by water temperature and not the calendar. I look for the first significant drop in the water temperature to trigger the walleye bite. Even though walleyes are active in summer, after the water temperature drops the bite becomes more intense. You will still get the occasional short strike but they happen less often, and if you miss one fish another is close by.

The first place I check out in the early fall is creek channels and slough edges which are usually loaded with baitfish. In fall, a creek will start to see a migration of baitfish out of the creek into the main river channel. Weeds begin to die off in a slough as the days become shorter, and, as the water temperature drops, baitfish move out along the edge of the slough. Food is plentiful, but walleyes will share this banquet with bass and northern pike.

A slough is productive regardless of the water level. When fishing a slough for walleye it is important to concentrate on the edge where the weeds end and the river channel breaks to deep water. Sloughs that fan out across shallow water will attract pike and bass but only straggler walleyes. Use your trolling motor to hold you parallel to the slough and cast crankbaits as tightly to the weeds as possible. After you make a few casts with the crankbait, even if you catch some walleyes, switch over to live bait. Use either a jig and minnow or a red tail chub.

A creek channel is best fished when the water is high or rising. If there is a moderate amount of water flowing through the creek, baitfish will be present, but not in large numbers. However, any increase in the flow of water in the creek can change the amount of baitfish holding at the edge of the creek channel. Walleyes will feed primarily early and late in the day while pike and bass will feed on the slough edges during the day.

Unlike spring when walleyes will migrate up a creek to spawn, in the fall they will hold on the edge of the creek and, except for extremely high water, won't venture into the creek. Start fishing with a shallow running minnow imitation crankbait on the sides of the creek where it enters the river. Top crankbait colors are perch, chartreuse and black/silver. If there are weeds on either side of the creek channel you can fish the area like a slough.

At any given time, the bulk of the walleyes will hold in a deep hole which is usually associated with a creek channel. Use your electronics to mark walleyes and position your boat directly over them, then vertical jig with a jig and minnow. The big difference when vertical jigging in the fall is in your choice of minnow. In fall, use larger minnows since walleyes are looking for a larger profile bait. If you have short strikes, then let the walleye take the minnow for a few seconds before you set the hook.

On many occasions anchoring is more productive than vertical jigging. Anchoring the boat allows the angler to let the bait sit in the hole for a long period of time without moving it. This dead sticking tactic will catch a lot of big walleyes that can be passed up by an angler who is vertical jigging. I use this tactic a lot while guiding due to its simplicity especially when there are more than two people in the boat.

Just as in the spring, I never pass up a bridge in the fall. While walleye will relate to a bridge regardless of the season, bridges commonly attract big walleyes in the fall. The only time fall walleyes don't seem to relate to a bridge is during periods of low water. If they are found in the vicinity of a bridge in low water, it is around the center columns in deep water. Walleyes will hold tight to the base of the structure and are usually in a negative mood and tough to catch.

Bring on rising water and you can expect some phenomenal action. After a few days of rain, look for baitfish and walleye to be pushed downstream. A bridge is a large obstruction that can attract all types of fish. Smallmouth bass will usually ride high in the water column and suspend off the structure while walleyes will hold deeper and tight to structure. If the bait does not get down you will catch lots of smallmouth but no walleyes. In order to get the bait through that school of hungry smallmouth use a heavier jig. Use between a 1/4 or 3/8 ounce jig and tip it with a medium sized red tail chub. Top jig colors are orange, chartreuse, yellow and hot pink. If possible, hold your boat in the current with your trolling motor, but if you can't then anchor.

One of my favorite spots when looking for big fall walleyes is steep shoreline with downed wood. Besides being steep, prime areas will drop to at least 15 feet of water. Shallow wooded shorelines might hold bass, but don't expect to find walleyes. Big walleyes will scatter along the wood and they will make vertical movements towards the surface to feed on baitfish holding in the wood. I have caught many large walleyes just inches from the shoreline tight to the wood.

Early morning and late afternoon are the best time to look for walleyes holding tight to shoreline wood. Crankbaits can be very effective, but I have had my best success with a jig and minnow or a red tail chub on a plain hook. Cast the jig and let it fall, and once you feel wood or the bottom, if you don't get snagged, give the jig a few twitches. Let the jig drop again and when you again feel the bottom, recast. It is important not to waste too much time fishing the bottom, but concentrate on the ledge and the wood. During the day, look for bass and pike to be relating to these same areas.

30" fall walleye caught with a chub

Rig the chub on a number 1 or 1/0 kahle hook with a few split shots clinched about 18 inches up from the line. Make your cast tight to the shoreline and watch your line for any movement. If you see movement as soon as the bait enters the water, give the minnow a few seconds and then set the hook. Don't retrieve the minnow, but let it drop along the ledge, keeping an eye on the line for movement. If the conditions will allow, I will often drag a minnow on the bottom and cast the shoreline. This allows you to cover the entire area efficiently.

During the day, walleyes will fan out along the bottom and both vertical jigging and dragging a live bait rig will work. When dragging a live bait rig, use enough weight to keep the bait on the bottom. If the bait does not ride on the bottom, you won't catch too many walleyes. If you mark big fish on your locator, slow down and fish as slowly as possible. If you mark walleye and are not catching them, toss out the anchor and sit a while.

Flowages are most productive once the water temperature drops below 55 degrees. Once the water drops below 55 degrees, the weeds start to die off and walleyes relate to off shore structure. Walleyes relate to humps as they did in the summer, but they will use the deepest humps in the flowage. One of my favorite humps tops off at 15 feet below the surface and the front of the hump drops sharply to 35 feet of water. The other three sides of the hump taper down to 20 to 25 foot depths. Humps that don't have at least one side with a steep drop off are not that productive in the fall.

Start looking for walleyes atop the hump since they will be the most active. If I locate walleyes on the top of the hump I rely on my anchor to keep me on the spot. Cast and retrieve a 1/4 or 3/8 ounce jig and work it slowly over the hump. The cast and retrieve presentation is more deadly than vertical jigging since walleyes relating to a deep hump don't seem to want to rise up in the water column to strike a bait. As usual, I rig up a big chub and dead stick it on another line.

If walleyes are not atop the hump they will hold on the steep side of the hump. Walleyes will be tough to mark on your locator since they hold tight to the rocks or the bottom. This is a tough area to fish since besides being tough to locate, walleyes also don't seem to want to move. It will take lots of patience but if you are willing to stick it out, you can catch a few lunker walleyes.

My favorite tactic is to position my boat over the steep drop off and drop a big red tail chub over the side of the boat with a slip bobber. I hook the chub through the back and use only as many small split shots as needed. Set one slip bobber so the chub swims about one foot off the bottom and another so the chub swims about three feet off the bottom. I always keep one rod with the chub one foot of the bottom but randomly raise and lower the other line. By raising and lowering the slip bobber, you are able to catch walleyes that are migrating along the drop off. As I said, this method takes patience but it is very deadly.

Lunker walleye from a deep hump

One thing is for certain, when November arrives fisherman will find no lines at the boat landing. You will be able to head out to your favorite lake and probably have the water to yourself. November can be trophy time but it can also be one of the most frustrating and unpredictable times in which to fish. The late fall period is one time of year when fishing the proper lake is a must. Lakes that are tough in summer and early fall can be hot before ice up.

First off, we must determine which lakes are going to be the most productive. Clear water is a must for consistent fishing. The clearer and more infertile the water the greater your odds will be to land a trophy fish. Many clear lakes will have trophy class fish, but their numbers can be low. These clear lakes have a depleted forage base and large predator fish are on the prowl. Darker and moderately fertile lakes will have a greater abundance of forage and large predator fish are less apt to cooperate. Flowages in particular, which are steady producers most of the year, see only limited November action unless there is a limited forage base or a migration downstream above a dam.

Besides clear water the second important factor is rocks. On many clear lakes rocks are the only form of structure available on the lake. By November the weeds are dead and don't play an important part in fish location. The last remaining forage can be found relating to rock. By rocks, I am referring to both offshore structure and shoreline rocks. These same areas may only hold a few transit fish throughout summer and early fall. On certain days you will find fish relating to the rocks but they don't hold there for extended periods of time; basically they move in and out. Once the temperature drops below 48 degrees more and more forage fish move into the rocks. Since all types of forage fish move into the rocks, expect all types of predator fish to be present. Walleye, musky, smallmouth, largemouth and pike may all be present on the same structure. Not only will you find an abundance of fish, but trophy fish as well.

A lake does not need to have an abundance of rock to be productive. If too much rock is present in the lake finding fish can be difficult. Look for lakes with only a few rock piles or rocky points. A fisherman must also understand that all rocks are different. Your favorite rock shoreline that held fish in the spring might not be productive in November. However, on other lakes the same rock shoreline can be productive. Rock shorelines with access to deep water are typically the most productive. Shallow rock flats are only productive if this is the only rock structure available within the lake.

On multi-species lakes each type of predator fish will relate to rock structure differently. If smallmouth bass are present they will usually suspend off the rocks, while walleyes will be holding tightly to the rocks. If smallmouth bass are not present in the lake then walleyes can both suspend and hold tight to the rocks. The walleyes holding tight to the rocks will be more aggressive. Walleyes will also relate to much deeper structure than smallmouth. It is common to find walleyes as deep as 35 feet on many clear water lakes. Pike and musky can also be feeding off rock structure although they are solitary fish.

On many lakes, wood is the key to late fall walleye location. This wood can be downed shoreline wood or fish cribs. Fish cribs in particular can be a big walleye magnet in the fall. Most lakes that have fish cribs have very little natural structure so the cribs are the only game in town. The lake I mentioned in Chapter 4 is a good example. By late fall big walleyes stack up on the deep edge of the crib like cordwood. A large red tail chub or sucker suspended a few inches above a walleye is difficult for a walleye to pass up.

Just like earlier in the season, you will need to approach the fish crib with caution so you don't spook the fish.

Both clear and overcast days can be productive but overcast days are the most ideal. On overcast days walleyes can be active throughout the day. It is common to see sporadic feeding sprees that are short but intense. They will bite like crazy then close their mouths. However, just when you think it is over and decide to head for the boat landing, they turn on again for another feeding binge. If you hang in there, your odds are greatly increased for a shot at a trophy.

Limit of *eating size* November walleyes

Clear skies are less desirable, but under a stable weather pattern walleyes will show some activity. Mid-day fishing can be good, but look for the late afternoon to be the most productive. By late fall the days are short and the sun seems to go behind the trees in a matter of minutes. Without the twilight, when walleyes decide to feed, it can happen fast. This feeding binge can be fantastic, but it is usually short lived. Bluebird skies after a front passes can mean tough fishing for all species.

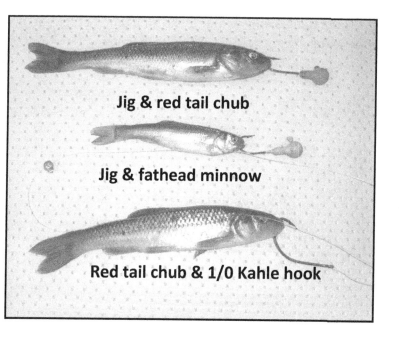

Jig & red tail chub

Jig & fathead minnow

Red tail chub & 1/0 Kahle hook

As far as presentation goes, when fishing clear water lakes I rely almost entirely on live bait. Since trolling is not allowed on most northern Wisconsin lakes, live bait is my only option. Even if trolling is allowed, it is tough to troll a bait in deep cover. Red tail chubs are the number one bait and I fish them either on a plain Aberdeen hook or with a jighead. Usually, I use both presentations. I will cast and retrieve or vertical jig with a jig and chub, and dead stick a big chub a few feet above the structure I am fishing. Most of the time, I catch the smaller walleyes with the jig and chub and the big walleye on the dead stick.

Once November arrives don't put the boat away. Remember, this is trophy time; take advantage of every last minute. It may seem like punishment at times, but once you get a big fish on your line you'll quickly forget all your discomfort. Even if it is a bit uncomfortable, remember that it is going to be a long winter and a long time before you hit open water.

Chapter Eight
Canadian Walleyes

One thing I have learned over my 25 years of guiding is to never bet on a sure thing. Anglers who get locked into only one or very few presentations will only have moderate success. Sure they may catch that occasional trophy fish but they will also get skunked more often than they will admit. The more versatile the angler is the more fish they will put in the boat.

Being versatile also means fishing different waters; not only different types of water in your area, but different locations as well. It is a proven fact that every time you fish a new body of water you will pick up a few tricks that you can use back on your home water. That is why regardless of what your wife says, you need to go on more fishing trips to new locations to further enhance your education. Sounds like as good a reason as any to take a vacation and if you are a walleye fishermen, there is no better place to go than to Canada.

Those anglers who are after trophy walleye would fare better concentrating on the Great Lakes. The Great Lakes keep producing huge numbers of trophy walleye and due to their vast size, depleting these fisheries of their trophy potential is a difficult scenario to envision. However, if all you are after is catching fish the Great Lakes don't offer much for aesthetics. Be prepared to see lots of open water and the occasional passing of another boat. If the fishing is slow, you are in for a very long day.

Canadian lakes offer excellent walleye fisheries and most of them are located in a real wilderness setting. Wilderness is one of the most misused words in our vocabulary. For example some city people think that wilderness is a 40 acre plot of woods with no electricity. My idea of wilderness is a place that is unspoiled with little if any sign of human habitation. You might be able to enjoy a few modern conveniences at a lodge or in your cabin, but cell phones, computers, and TV's are nowhere to be found. You should be able to drive your boat for miles without seeing any shoreline development. Basically you have nothing else to do but go fishing.

Besides offering a wilderness experience, Canadian lakes offer both high numbers of fish and quality walleyes to boot. Even with the odds in their favor given the pres-

Nice Canadian walleye

ence of so many quality fish, anglers with high expectations but limited experience may struggle to be successful. They might have a favorite bait that has worked in the past and they think their favorite bait will work on every lake they fish. These are the guys that go home and blame the lake for their lack of success instead of blaming themselves; not that the average angler has an ego problem, it's just that far too many of us anglers are prone to exaggerate our ability

    Fishing a Canadian lake is no different than fishing a lake in the upper Midwest. Anglers often need to refine their presentations to conform to the individual water they are fishing. Even on lakes with excellent walleye populations it is important to be prepared to use several different presentations. If you are searching for trophy walleyes it is even more important. I have great success fishing Canadian walleyes, but I can assure you that there are times when the fishing is tough and in those times you need to pull out all the stops.

Being a guide in northern Wisconsin I have been fishing for weed walleyes for as long as I can remember. My experiences fishing for weed walleyes has enabled me to catch many large Canadian walleyes on lakes where big walleyes seemed to be rare. However, on many Canadian lakes few anglers take advantage of this weed walleye bite. With many Canadian lakes seeing limited fishing pressure, the weed related walleye sees no pressure at all. Not only can anglers find action by fishing the weeds but hawg walleyes can be present as well. I must admit that I too did not take advantage of these weed walleyes for a number of years. While musky fishing in deep weedlines I had several 28-inch plus walleye attack my crankbaits and jerkbaits. It took a while for the light bulb to turn on in my head but after seeing a walleye in the 12-pound class hammer my musky bait I realized that this was no accident.

One summer, this weed bite saved the trip not only for me but for most of the people staying at the lodge. The fishing was tough and people were having trouble catching walleyes. It did not seem to matter where or how people were fishing, they were just not catching any walleye. The biggest problem was that nobody could find them. Everyone fished deep water, rock reefs, steep rock shoreline, and all the usual summer hotspots. The guests were not happy and the owner of the lodge was nowhere to be found. Since I had no one to go to for advice, I knew I had to figure something out for myself. As they say, "If you want something done, do it yourself!"

One morning I told my friend Ed that we were only going to fish the weeds. Since our success rate was far from impressive and Ed had limited fishing experience, he really did not care where we fished. Ed was along for the ride, and although he did like to fish, he was content with just being there. However, I was frustrated that I could not figure out how to catch the walleyes in that particular lake. I had fished the lake several times and knew it had a good walleye fishery.

The first place I decided to fish was a weedline where I had seen a big walleye hit my jerkbait while musky fishing the previous year. That big walleye that was in the weeds was on the feed. It was not chasing small minnows and the fact that it had hit my jerkbait meant that it was probably feeding on the same forage that the muskies were eating. The weeds were on the edge of a huge bay that was the size of some of the lakes that I fished back home. On the edge of one bay the water dropped from eight to twenty feet, and to my way of thinking the spot had big fish written all over it. I told Ed that the fish had to be there and all we needed to do was figure out how to catch them.

Since trolling is legal on most Canadian lakes I opted to troll medium running crankbaits. I tied on a perch pattern crankbait and gave Ed a black and silver pattern crankbait. We were flat line trolling, nothing fancy but yet very deadly in its simplicity. Speed is always important when trolling and even more so when you are searching for fish. A slightly faster trolling speed will trigger a strike from a neutral fish and attract them from a farther distance than a slower trolling speed. We trolled the edge of the weeds at a fairly fast pace for about twenty minutes when Ed yelled, "Fish on."

By the bend in Ed's rod, I knew it was a big fish. As the reel screamed, Ed had all he could do to hold onto the rod. We both thought the fish was a muskie or a big northern pike. Eventually Ed started to gain on the walleye and as it got close to the boat I was ready to net the fish. Much to our surprise and delight, it was not a musky or northern pike but a huge walleye. Ed did a good job of fighting the big walleye but when he brought it boatside it took another run and snapped his line. We both knew that that was probably the fish of the trip.

Ed with a 25 inch walleye

We repeated the trolling pattern and in about five minutes I tied into a nice fish but I knew it was nothing to brag about. However, it did result in the first legal walleye of the trip. We put the walleye in the live well and continued our trolling pattern. We had found the pattern and the rest of the morning caught at least 25 walleyes from that weedline. If we had boated that big walleye it would have been an ideal morning.

After we ate lunch, I told Ed I knew of another spot very similar to the one we had just fished and as things turned out the next spot was no different from the first. Trolling the weedline produced a bunch of 16-24 inch walleyes. We had to cover a huge area since the walleyes were scattered. If we would have held tight in the spot after we caught a walleye, we would not have caught very many walleyes.

The walleyes were on the move and we were moving along the weedline making connecting with fish inevitable. Given this situation, trolling a crankbait is the ideal presentation.

Trolling is not the only presentation that will catch weed related Canadian walleyes. Since we are dealing with aggressive walleye there is often no need for live bait. Cast parallel to the weeds with a leadhead jig and four inch twister tail. Make sure when working the jig and twister tail you keep the bait tight to the weedline and let it drop to the base of the weeds. The big walleyes will hit the bait on the drop. If you fail to boat walleyes or the action suddenly slows then tip the jig with either a nightcrawler or minnow. The more presentations you use while in the weeds the more and larger walleyes you will catch.

I could not wait to get back to the lodge to see how the other anglers had done. Were the walleyes active that day and everyone brought in fish, or did we figure out a pattern and end up being the only ones who caught fish? Not that Ed and I were thinking about bragging, but it is human nature for anglers to want to compare their results with others.

We got back at the dock and placed the walleyes on a stringer. Normally we would not have kept our limit of walleyes, but with as slow as the fishing had been, we did not know if we would see any more walleye. As we headed for the fish cleaning house, we drew a crowd and it seemed everyone in the camp came down to see our catch. It was like a circus as people who we did not even know were taking pictures and treating us like kings. I even had a guy offer to clean the walleyes for me. Somehow I had the feeling that if I would have let the guy clean the fish the package would have been on the light side!

That night at the lodge I brought my crankbaits and a lake map and gave a mini seminar. It was evident that this was the only pattern that was working since only a few other walleyes had been caught by people staying at the lodge. My advice was well taken and most of the guests at the lodge caught walleyes the rest of the week. The only problem for Ed and I was that we did reveal our spot and it was loaded with boats. That forced us to go musky fishing the rest of the week and, happily, I ultimately connected with a 45 incher.

The advantage to fishing for weed walleyes is that they are aggressive. Once you locate weed walleyes they will usually remain there for the immediate future and you will be able to return on a daily basis. There is no need for finesse presentations to take deep-water walleyes. Find a weedbed at the edge of a bay with access to deep water and big walleyes should be close by.

For consistent action on a daily basis it is hard to beat backtrolling with a nightcrawler harness. The most important aspect of backtrolling is to keep the bait as vertical as possible. By keeping your crawler harness vertical not only will you trigger more strikes but also snags are less frequent. When a strike is detected wait a few seconds and use a slow direct hook set. A crawler harness requires a more restrained set allowing the walleye a few seconds to engulf the bait.

Many of the areas in which I like to back troll in summer are steep rock shelves where vertical jigging would have been tough if not impossible. Walleyes will hold tight to the rocks and the combination of the nightcrawler and the spinner is tough to beat. As far as tackle goes I was just using a medium action six foot six rod.

Backtrolling will catch lots of walleyes but don't adopt it as your sole presentation. Many times an angler will catch a big walleye and keep backtrolling and catch nothing. By switching to a jigging presentation you may catch a few

Jerry & Joe with a a bunch of Canadian walleyes

more big walleyes. Experiment until you find the proper jig weight. If the jig is too heavy you will snag up often, but if you use too light a jig the bait won't hit bottom. Use either a jig with a crawler or a jig and twister tail. As far as color goes I have good success with both orange and chartreuse, but bring along an assortment of different colors.

When you are searching for active fish while fishing rock ledges you will need to cover a lot of water and trolling a deep diving crankbait is the best way to locate walleyes. When you connect, toss out a floating marker and continue to make passes past the marker. Unlike weed walleyes which can scatter, rock related walleyes tend to bunch up. However, though they bunch up they can be at different depths in the water column. It is important to cover a variety of depths until you connect with walleyes. It is typical to have two different crankbaits running at different depths and both will be catching walleyes.

Color can be just as important as the depth. Walleyes will hone in on a specific forage and will hit a crankbait that resembles the forage while refusing any other color pattern. Besides matching the forage, another tip is to use black/silver patterns on overcast days and on bright days use either a fire tiger or perch pattern. If the lake has a whitefish or ciscoe population, try blue/ silver or highly reflective pattern baits. After you have caught the active walleyes by trolling, start jigging.

On many Canadian Lakes the key to catching trophy walleyes in summer is fishing a reef. A good rule to follow is the deeper and more isolated the reef is the larger the walleyes will be. You may not catch numbers of walleyes on a deep reef adjacent to deep water but it may hold a hawg. Here again a variety of presentations is needed to effectively fish a reef. You can vertical jig the top, backtroll the edges or forward troll deep diving crankbaits over the top. Make sure you use all your options when fishing a reef.

I always say that I never saw a reef that I did not like. I don't care where the reef is located on a lake, at any given time there are walleye either on top of the reef or in close proximity. The problem is that even though there are walleyes in the vicinity, they do not always cooperate. In fact, fishing a reef can be frustrating since most anglers don't know when to let it go and move on. Many times marking a lot of walleyes with your electronics can be a bad thing as anglers spend too much time trying to catch them.

I fell into this rut many times through the years since I was determined to catch walleyes off of my favorite reef. The reef was situated in a neck down area of the lake that anglers would pass through as they dispersed throughout the lake. For a wilderness lake the area did get a fair amount of boat traffic. However, just as anglers would zip from one end of the lake to the other, so would the walleyes. So it is easy to understand why at any given time, the reef would hold walleyes, as long as there was not a big muskie on the prowl.

As walleyes would migrate through the neck down area, the reef was not an obstruction, but rather a restaurant. The reef topped out at 14 feet below the surface; on two sides it dropped to 30 feet, while one side dropped to 50 feet and the other side to 20 feet. It had big walleye written all over it. I think that some of the walleyes were using the reef as a holding area and others were using it to feed. The new arrivals to the reef would pig out on a variety of baitfish and then hold tight on the deep edge of the reef. Due to these movements, the major feeding on the reef would occur from mid-day through the evening. There never seemed to be any active walleyes on the reef early in the day. I spent many a morning giving the reef a try, thinking that a few big walleyes would be hunting for an early meal.

Backtrolling spinner rigs, drifting live bait rigs and vertical jigging were all deadly tactics on the reef. When using live bait rigs, a night crawler on a slip sinker rig with a floating jighead was my most productive tactic. The floating jighead enabled the crawler to float above the rocks and within easy striking distance of a hungry walleye. If I fished the rig with a plain hook, the crawler would hug the bottom and I would get strikes from small walleyes and perch. These smaller fish can be annoying and will clean you out of nightcrawlers.

Of course, when you are looking for walleyes a good set of electronics is a must. Even if you are using a lodge boat, invest in a portable locator. Many lodges put electronics on their boats but they are the generic variety and while they will mark structure, these generic locators won't distinguish baitfish or the size of the predator fish. Don't just look for big walleyes on your locator since they could be tight to the rocks on the reef or along the edges. Look for baitfish. If baitfish are present, a big walleye should be close by as well. Make sure that you also search the adjacent water for suspended baitfish and walleyes since walleyes have a tendency to suspend off structure.

By utilizing both backtrolling crawler harnesses, vertical jigging and forward trolling crankbaits you can make walleye fishing a learning experience. Remember there is always room to add a new weapon to your arsenal. By changing your presentations you will finally land that trophy fish of a lifetime. And just as an aside, I would highly recommend a trip to the far north at least once in your life.

Chapter Nine

Hard Water Walleyes

Walleye are one of the most difficult fish to put a handle on during the hard water period. At times the action can be fast and furious while at other times even catching a 12 incher is tough. Just as during the open water period, timing is the key. Some lakes will be productive from first ice through the end of the season, while other lakes will have high and low fishing periods, and others just don't seem to produce at all during winter.

If you are looking to fish the top peak period for winter walleye, it is hard to beat first ice. Up here in the Northwood's we usually have some sort of hard water by early December and anglers can expect a time of plenty. Even if walleyes refuse to hit your bait, anglers have many options at first ice since there always seems to be something biting. They can fish tip ups for walleye and northern pike or opt to jig for walleyes and panfish in the weeds. The only problem many people have during the first ice period is deciding for what specie to fish.

However, it may not be as simple as going on the ice, drilling a few holes and catching fish. Each lake or flowage is different and anglers must adapt accordingly. Not only is all water different but panfish and predator fish will have different feeding patterns depending on the type of water you are fishing. Once you understand the first ice period, you can experience productive fishing, although you will have to deal with changing weather conditions which have an effect on fishing.

Concentrate on the actual flowage itself, since the upper riverine sections on the flowage seldom see safe ice. Always put safety first when ice fishing; flowages in particular require an extra bit of caution. Due to the danger of the current, anglers should restrict their fishing to the access sites and not venture out into the main river channel. Even if we experience sub-zero temperatures for long periods of time, river ice is never completely safe.

Flowages in general offer good walleye fishing throughout the winter. Many of these flowages are small in size covering only a few hundred acres. Even though these flowages may not be large in size they contain good fishable walleye populations in winter. Besides catching legal 15 inchers, trophy walleye are present. The smaller the flowage is, the easier it will be to locate winter walleyes.

Small to mid-sized flowages are the first waters to have safe ice. With their many shallow back bays flowages can be covered with six inches of ice while a deep clear lake just a few miles down the road still has open water. Flowage walleyes are notorious for going on the prowl in shallow water at first ice. When walleyes go on the feed even a poorly placed presentation will catch walleyes. But for the most part, to consistently catch first ice walleye you will need to refine your presentation as well as focus on fishing in the right areas.

I have fished many medium sized flowages over the years and for the most part winter walleye patterns are the same. First ice can offer exceptional action. Walleye move into shallow bays and feed heavily, especially at night. Big walleye are caught quit easily by even novice anglers. The first ice bite generally lasts only a few weeks on flowages and then walleye move deep. On one of my favorite flowages, the big walleye bite would last for three weeks at the most. Once the walleye bite stopped it was tough to catch one legal walleye in a day or night of fishing. Most anglers forget about walleyes and spend the winter in pursuit of other species.

Flowages with good weed growth are also worth fishing. Weeds hold hoards of baitfish that concentrate in small areas once ice covers a back bay. All the remaining baitfish will hold on the edge of the weeds so it is important that anglers know the exact location of the weedline. You will need to drill a series of holes to establish the weedline. Forget about fishing well into the weeds unless they are cabbage weed and the weeds are still green. If the weeds are milfoil or coontail they will be void of life once the ice covers the flowage since oxygen levels will be too low to support life.

First ice walleyes can be caught by both jigging and with tip ups. The preferred method will depend on the individual flowages. Jigging is fun and can produce lots of action but if you are looking for a trophy walleye it's hard to beat a large golden shiner on a tip up. Even in flowages, big walleyes are most active after dark, so pattern your fishing accordingly. Try fishing during the day for eating size walleyes and then, after dark, fish for that trophy. It is important to keep the right walleyes when ice fishing. Keeping 15-20 inch fish for a meal is fine but release larger walleyes unless they are going to be mounted; this protects the fish population.

In Wisconsin, we are allowed three lines per angler. Since we are allowed such generous regulations, you might as well utilize them. If you are fishing with a few partners, you can cover large areas effectively. Set tip ups both along the weedline and in deeper water. Next, drill a series of holes along the weedline for jigging. After a series of holes are drilled anglers can jump from hole to hole and with the use of a portable locator, they can cover all depths in the water column. With each angler using a different presentation, you won't pass up too many walleyes.

If you are looking for wallhanger walleyes, look for shallow weedy bays on the edge of the main river channel. These are big fish spots in the fall and big walleyes will remain tight to the river channel throughout most of the winter. Walleyes will make periodic movements to the weedlines to feed and then move back to the edge of the river channel. These movements can occur at the strangest times making their movements impossible to pattern. Wall-eyes can go on the feed at anytime and without any warning, so be prepared and stick it out.

Some of the best action can occur in the middle of the day under bright sunny skies. I remember one February day when I fished a flowage for about three hours without any action at all. My partner and I figured the weather was too nice and we were just about ready to wrap things up when a flag went up on a tip up set in 25 feet of water. As I approached the tip up, I remember thinking that it would be no big deal if it was a false alarm since I was planning on picking up the tip up. Usually when a flag goes up, an angler is all pumped up. However, I remember that I did not have even the slightest adrenalin flow as I approached the tip up.

When I got to the tip up and saw the spool spinning, I knew that it was a serious fish. After I set the hook I knew it was a serious fish and yelled to my partner that I had a fish on. The one thing about tip up fishing is that you are really never sure of the size of the fish until it gets close to the surface. As I pulled in the line the fish felt heavier and I thought for sure it was a big northern pike. But as I pulled up some more line and saw the white tip of the tail I knew it was a big walleye. Soon there was a 28 inch walleye lying on the ice. Since the fish was too big to keep, I quickly released it back into the hole.

Just as my partner mentioned how we thought we should hang around a bit longer, I gazed at the weedline and saw three more flags from our tip ups. So here we were at high noon, in bright sun with three flags and only two anglers. Having to choose between one of two flags after hours of no flags is a welcome sight for any ice fisherman. The trick is to pick the flag that has the largest fish on the end of the line.

Well, we got lucky since we were able to retrieve all of the fish on the tip ups. They were all walleyes between 16 and 18 inches, making them the perfect size for a meal. We unhooked the fish and reset the tip ups as fast as possible. It did not take long for the flags to go up and once again we had three more legal walleyes. We repeated the procedure which resulted in three more legal walleyes. This is simply incredible action regardless of where you are fishing.

The action shut down after the last three fish and we hung around for another thirty or forty minutes. We did not want to leave and were hoping for another feeding binge to occur at anytime. Much to our dismay, it looked like it was not in the cards. Nonetheless, we were happy with our nine walleyes. I don't know what impressed me the most, the fact that we had caught nine legal walleyes, or the fact that we had caught them at high noon in about forty five minutes. I never did figure out what had caused the walleyes to go on the rampage at mid-day. All I know is that I have never had action like that again nor do I expect to do so any time soon.

On some flowages walleye movements will be dictated by the amount of water moving through the flowage. If the flow is moderate to light many walleyes will remain deep. However, find a flowage with some moving water and you will find shallow walleye. Walleyes will try to avoid any current in the winter. Besides walleyes any forage fish will also move shallow due to the current. The problem is that in winter a change in the current flow is rare. If you happen to be in the right place at the right time, you can clean house.

Since we don't usually have any large changes in the water flow in the flowage, even a slight increase in the flow can spark walleye feeding. This slight flow increase will happen most often in late February. By late February the days are longer and the sun is high, and even though the air temperature is only slightly above freezing, a great deal of melting can occur. As the snow starts to melt, water seeps into the upper reaches of the flowage and can increase the current just enough to stimulate a late afternoon walleye bite. It is a deep water bite with walleye feeding on small perch that are pushed away from deep wood by the current.

Even though these deep water walleyes are feeding on perch, a golden shiner on a tip up is the bait of choice. Set the tip ups a few feet away from the wood and about three feet off the bottom. Walleyes will move up to strike the tip up, but they won't move down in the water column to strike a bait. Prior to the current increase, they are holding on the bottom, tight to the wood, and as the current increases they rise up about one foot and move away from the wood. A properly placed tip up will be right in the strike zone.

If you are fishing with a few friends, try to set tip ups over as many different areas that contain deep wood as possible. Walleyes holding on deep stumps on a mud flat can be like finding a needle in a haystack for even the most seasoned angler. While I can easily locate deep wood, I know the water I am fishing like the back of my hand. This is another situation where a GPS will greatly aid a fisherman since the wood can be locked in the GPS during open water. The ideal situation is to use the GPS to locate the wood and your locater to set your tip up to the exact depth.

Large deep flowages tend to be productive in the coldest part of winter when fishing on shallow flowages comes to a halt. In fact, on one of my favorite winter flowages, I have had great success within walking distance of a boat landing. On this particular flowage, just out from the landing is an old railroad bridge and the south shoreline is an excellent area for evening walleye. Use tip ups with shiners and set them in 10-12 feet of water. During the day, work the deep edge of the shoreline with tip ups.

The same flowage has an island just west of the bridge that can also be good for walleye. I would set tip ups in 8-12 feet of water and jig along the deeper edges. At dusk look for any weed edge to attract feeding walleyes. If you are looking for large walleye, concentrate on the edge of the river channel. When fishing the edge of the river channel concentrate on submerged wood and rock. Even though the best action is at first ice a good evening bite is common throughout winter.

When fishing flowages in mid to late winter, wise anglers will utilize both jigging and fishing tip ups. It is a foolish angler who goes on the ice and only uses one presentation. Set one tip up at the point where the weedline tapers near deep water, making sure it is out of any current. If you want to set another tip up hold it tight to the weedline. After you drill a series of holes along the weedline start jigging. I jig with both spoons and jigging Rapalas. On most of the flow-ages I fish spoons produce the best. Another option often overlooked by anglers is jigging with smaller tear drops and minnow head jigheads. A minnow or wax worm attached to one of these jigs is deadly when the bite is light. Last year I had great success with the tear drops and minnow head jigs.

Natural lakes are great at first ice although you might not see a feeding rampage in shallow water. Clear water lakes in particular having limited structure and weeds will find walleyes bunching up. Once you locate a school they can be easily caught. The same lake however can be tough to fish by mid-winter. While I like fishing natural lakes, given the option I prefer a flowage for consistent walleye action.

Shallow weedy natural lakes are not known for growing oversized walleyes, but they can be consistent producers of eating sized walleyes in the winter. Like shallow flowages, peak walleye activity will occur at first ice as walleyes move into the shallows to feed. The water on most natural lakes is clearer than flowages making them ideal for a night bite.

Just as with flowages, walleyes can move very shallow at first ice. The rule of thumb is to set your tip ups in as shallow water as the weeds will allow. On some lakes shallow weeds will be too dense and they will deter walleyes from moving shallow. Drill a series of holes to look for changes in the density of the weeds. Once you locate fishable weeds start fishing from that point while gradually moving deeper. Even though you are fishing at night, it is easier to locate the weeds when you still have some daylight.

Clear infertile natural lakes usually have a reputation for producing quality walleyes during the winter. Hard water anglers usually don't catch high numbers of walleyes but these lakes give up many a 10 pound walleye in winter. In fact, on some Northwood's lakes big walleyes are prone to overharvest in winter. Those big walleyes that spend most of the open water season chasing ciscoes become less gun shy in winter, so it is important that anglers practice restraint and release those trophy walleyes which are typically females full of eggs.

The average deep clear lake will take much longer to freeze and the first ice may occur as much as three weeks after a shallow lake freezes over. The bite starts later in the season and continues on into mid-winter. The bite then continues but anglers need to adapt to walleye location. Early in the ice season walleyes relate to weeds and late in the season they relate to off shore structure. Whether you are fishing at early ice or late ice, you will need to concentrate your efforts to fishing at night or on overcast days. Very seldom will walleyes on deep clear lakes become active on bright days.

At first ice walleye in deep clear lakes will search out weeds just as in flowages and shallow lakes. The big difference is that they do not necessarily move as shallow. How shallow they will move will depend on the available forage. On deep clear lakes baitfish, which include perch, will stack up along the weedlines, which on many lakes can be as deep as 12 feet. The larger walleyes will move no shallower than needed to find a meal, so anglers should concentrate on these deeper weeds if they are looking for larger walleyes and move a bit shallower if they are looking for eating sized walleyes.

After two or three weeks the weedline bite comes to an abrupt halt and walleyes go on the move. Some of them will suspend and chase ciscoes or whitefish while others will relate to off shore structure. The suspended walleyes are catchable but they are like finding a needle in a haystack. Once you locate them and catch a few, if they move, good luck trying to relocate them. It can become a frustrating game of cat and mouse.

Off shore structure is easy to locate and it doesn't move. The ideal structure will be eight to fifteen feet below the surface. The actual location of the hump in the lake has little relevance as to its attraction to walleyes. As baitfish moves out of the shallows, the hump becomes the focal point for activity. Shallower humps will attract walleyes early in the winter especially if deeper humps are not available. However, by mid-winter most shallow humps are void of any aquatic life and are a waste of your time. If you are really looking for a wallhanger don't hesitate to fish humps as deep as 20 or 25 feet.

Fishing tip ups and jigging are both effective on these structure related walleyes and as usual, a combination of both presentations is in order. When fishing tip ups use large golden shiners and let them ride about a foot off the bottom regardless of the depth that you are fishing. A big walleye will hit a smaller shiner but a large shiner struggling atop a hump can attract a big walleye from a great distance. Jigging can also attract a big walleye but the walleye will eventually hit the tip up.

On many flowages and natural lakes, jigging spoons can produce nice catches of walleye each winter. The key to successful winter walleye fishing is in knowing the water you are fishing. Anglers need to be able to lock in on points, humps and drop offs. With many anglers using a GPS this is much easier than years past. All an angler has to do is lock in the points during the open water and bring along the GPS on the ice.

On larger lakes and flowages walleyes are mobile in winter as they follow the forage. These movements occur throughout the day and the season so spend some time with a jigging spoon acting as a search bait. Early in the hard water season walleye roam the weedlines and some anglers like to jig with a rattle spoon tipped with a minnow head. It is important to drill lots of holes and keep on the move. While keeping on the move is important, it is also important to work the spoon with patience, using a snap and flutter presentation. The slower you jig the spoon the better the results will be.

By mid-winter walleye continue to feed in the weeds but move to deeper structure during the day. Jigging spoons again are the bait of choice for locating these structure related walleye. Use the same snap and flutter presentation but also dead stick a jigging spoon with a shiner minnow rigged on the rear hook of the spoon. It is common for the snap and flutter motion to attract walleyes but the shiner triggers the actual strike. The shiner moves just enough to give the spoon some flash. Some anglers feel that the dead stick method is more productive than a tip up, being easier to change depth.

Winter cold fronts can slow down the bite so you will need to down size your spoon when needed. Over the years I have caught lots of walleyes while jigging for perch with smaller spoons. Downsizing your spoon after a cold front or when the bite slows down will improve your odds.

Walleyes do cooperate in winter but the bite can be very unpredictable. Some winters are better than others and people have been trying to figure this out for generations. The only thing that is for certain is that you can't catch them if you are not out on the ice.